CW01468243

John M. Scally
6/10/00

IN
CAMPBELTOWN
ONCE MORE

Boyhood memories of life in 'The Wee Toon'
during the fifties and sixties.

FREDDY GILLIES

By the same author

LIFE WITH THE COAL TAR
Stories from Campbeltown's West Coast fisherfolk.

LIFE ON GOD'S ISLAND
Stories from the Inner Hebridean Island of Gigha.

From book and craft shops or s.a.e. to: PO Box 3, Ellon,
AB41 9EA

ISBN: 0 – 905489 – 63 – 2

Copyright 2000 Famedram Publishers and Freddy
Gillies. Not to be reproduced in any form without written
authorisation from the publishers.

NORTHERN BOOKS FROM FAMEDRAM
ELLON AB41 9EA www.northernbooks.co.uk

PRINTED BY PRINTALL, GLASGOW.

ACKNOWLEDGEMENTS

I would like to thank the following people for their help in the
preparation of this book: George McMillan, Archie McCallum, John
McFadyen, Mrs Bella Ralston, Angus Morrison, Davie Brodie, all
Campbeltown; Mrs Greta Daniels, Glenbarr and Lachie Paterson,
Carradale. A special thanks to Sue Fortune, of the Campbeltown
Library and Museum.

Front cover: A typical summer scene in 1960's Campbeltown as holidaymakers stream off the Caledonian Steam Packet Company's *Waverley* at the Old Quay.

Back cover: An unusual shot of Campbeltown Town Hall taken in Kirk Street by local photographer John McFadyen.

CONTENTS

INTRODUCTION

Main Street, Campbeltown, Argyll, at ten minutes past ten on a mild Saturday morning in early 2000; I am conversing in the usual light-hearted manner with former Provost George McMillan outside his stationery shop at number 22.

George and I go back a long way, to the 1960's in fact, when his enthusiastic oratorical contributions as an Old Labour Town Councillor often provided the stimulus for impassioned debate on most topics concerning the general good of the town. This was manna to me in my role as a junior reporter on the old-style *Campbeltown Courier* and many eminently newsworthy articles, some of which made the national press, had their origins in the Town Hall council chamber.

As we talked, I let my gaze wander up and down the gently sloping broad ribbon of Main Street, slowly realising that what I was seeing - perhaps a dozen pedestrians dotted here and there on the pavements of this principal artery - was a sad indictment on modern-day Campbeltown.

Forty years ago at that time on a Saturday morning, as photographic evidence can easily verify, Main Street would have played host to a throng of people, contributing to a general scene of animation as they shopped, walked or engaged in small talk, accompanied by the merry ringing of cash register bells in the various commercial premises, including the main Post Office. I still cannot get used to the idea of a General Post Office being tucked away in the corner of a food supermarket.

I commented on this to George and our conversation took on an aura of nostalgia, perhaps even dolefulness, as we discussed the not-too-distant past. In our agreed opinion, Campbeltown was a much more vibrant and prosperous place in the fifties and sixties, even allowing for a massive decamp of more than 200 families to the giant steelworks of Stewart and Lloyd at Corby, Northants.

An elected Town Council ran the Royal Burgh and there were no big stores standing on its periphery to tear the heart out of the central shopping area.

A gazetteer published at the time had this, among other things, to say about the town: 'Campbeltown appears quite unexpectantly at the end of a scenic 40-mile drive along the Kintyre Peninsula's West Coast. It is a bustling, self-contained industrial town of nearly 7000 people, set in an area of outstanding natural beauty that is steeped in history. The Royal Burgh of Campbeltown is a worthwhile and interesting destination for the discerning traveller.'

My employment situation decrees that I cannot live in my native town, though I am fairly close at hand on the Isle of Gigha; but I am passionately fond of Campbeltown and the surrounding area. I mentioned the chat with George to another friend – also a 'Wee Toon' expatriate – and he suggested I write an account of life as it was during the period under discussion.

At first I discounted the idea, since I was, after all, only a child in the fifties. On considering the matter further, however, I was surprised by the clear memories I have of Campbeltown in that era. I seem to be blessed with a prodigious long-term memory and hold some perfectly vivid recollections of my surroundings when I was a toddler of less than three years old. Paradoxically, I have difficulty in remembering, for example, what was on the dinner table only two days ago!

The book is in no way intended to be a volume of historical record, but I have, nevertheless, striven for accuracy on this nostalgic journey down memory lane to look at a rather interesting period of Campbeltown's relatively recent past.

As well as covering the civic and commercial aspects, my own domestic circumstances are used as an example of a typically average Campbeltown family's lot. Similarly, autobiographical details serve merely to exemplify the life of an ordinary Campbeltown boy during my adolescence in the town at this time.

IN CAMPBELTOWN ONCE MORE
By Peter Gilchrist

Fare-ye-well my Nancy, a thousand times adieu,
Fare-ye-well my Nancy, but I must part from you,
I must part from you dear one, your'e the lassie I adore,
But we will live in hopes to meet in Cam'eltown once more

In Cam'eltown once more my boys,
In Cam'eltown once more,
Yes we will live in hopes to meet,
In Cam'eltown once more

Now the storm is raging, we can see it coming on,
The clouds are bent to westward, we can scarcely see the moon,
Our goodly ship is tossed about and our rigging's sadly torn,
But we will live in hope to meet in Cam'eltown once more

In Cam'eltown once more my boys etc.

Yes now the storm is raging, the waves are lashing high,
But bravely stems our gallant barque, the salt tear dims my eye,
The salt tear dims my eye my boys, but we will reach the shore,
And we will live in hopes to meet in Cam'eltown once more

In Cam'eltown once more my boys etc

Now the storm is ended and we are safe at last,
We've got the Trench Point now in view, Davaar Light we have
passed,
And soon we'll get our anchor down, when we get to the shore,
And we are back again my boys, in Cam'eltown once more,
In Cam'eltown once more my boys, in Cam'eltown once more,
And we are back again my boys, in Cam'eltown once more.

(Sung to the tune of The Holy Ground)

POPULATION

At the turn of the last century, Campbeltown was the biggest burgh in Argyll, with a population of 8300, although it hovered around the 10000 mark for a while during the boom years of the nineteenth century herring fishing industry. It was still a healthy 7172 in 1951 and, following the exodus to Corby, stood at 6523 in 1961.

However, the population has steadily declined over the years and the 1999 figures revealed that 5454 people were resident in the town. It has been forecast that the next census will show a further drop.

This worrying situation is in direct contrast to population counts in the two other main Argyll burghs of Oban and Dunoon, both of which have shown a slight upward trend.

Lochgilphead, too, has grown considerably, due mainly to the establishment of the Argyll and Bute Council headquarters there.

PART ONE

THE ROYAL BURGH OF CAMPBELTOWN

Ignavis Precibus Fortuna Repugnat
(FORTUNE HELPS THOSE THAT HELP
THEMSELVES)

Campbeltown 1950 – 1966

THE TOWN COUNCIL

When King William 3 created the Royal Burgh of Campbeltown by special charter in 1700, it was decreed that a Town Council should control its civic affairs. He included a particular prerequisite, which detailed the composition of such a body. Consequently, the original 17-strong Campbeltown Town Council consisted of a Provost, two Bailies, Burgh Treasurer, Dean of Guild and 12 councillors.

Nearly three centuries later, in May 1975, the last-ever meeting of the Town Council - sadly dissolved to make way for local government reorganisation - was held in the Town Hall chamber. This poignant occasion marked the end of 275 years of mainly unchanged council format and business procedure.

The Council elections were held each November until 1956, when the date was changed to the first Tuesday in May, and the fervour witnessed in Campbeltown during the run-up to voting day was evident to me even as a young boy. On election night a crowd assembled outside the Town Hall in Main Street, eager to hear the returning officer declare the results of the poll. Sometimes it was almost midnight before an announcement was made.

Successful candidates enjoyed a three-year term of office and the Council assembled on the Friday evening immediately following polling day. At this inaugural gathering – the forerunner of the monthly Monday evening Council meetings – various officials were appointed and nominees put forward to sit on a total of nine committees, each one with a different convener.

A traditional Kirkin' o' the Council took place two days later during Sunday worship, when the newly formed Council joined the congregation of, on a rotation basis, any one of the five presbyterian churches which were functioning then. The minister affiliated to the church in which this service took place became chaplain to the Council for the year and opened each monthly session with prayer.

The Provost, who was entitled to wear the magnificent gold chain of office, of course, filled the pre-eminent role. Following the dissipation of the Council, the Provost's chain, along with the two smaller Bailie's chains, were lodged in a bank at Lochgilphead, headquarters of Argyll and Bute Council. What will become of them in the future is a matter of some concern to many Campbeltonians, myself included.

The first Provost I remember was Archibald Keith, a local businessman. Surely his proudest day was the fabulous occasion in August 1958, when he welcomed Her Majesty the Queen on to a huge red-carpeted platform in Main Street. A visit to Campbeltown was included in her Royal Yacht Britannia cruise itinerary that year. As part of a massive crowd, I recall seeing Provost Keith attired in ermine robes and sporting the glittering chain. Despite a downpour towards the end of the proceedings, the day was unspoilt for thousands.

His successor was Anthony MacGrory, whose old established shop is still in business. He had two consecutive terms as Provost before being succeeded in 1965 by the articulate Duncan McMillan, who held the distinction of being the youngest councillor to hold the position. Provost McMillan also had the honour of being the first Labour councillor to be elevated to the office of civic leader.

Another Provost's perk was the privilege of having an ornate set of lamps erected outside his dwelling for the three-year period of service plus three years thereafter.

This practice was revived in the late fifties when a Campbeltown Grammar School technical teacher, James Edgar, bought Glenramskill House, the former home of a 1930's Provost Campbell. The lamps were surplus to requirements and were installed outside the residence of the Provost of the day, Anthony MacGrory, at *Glengarrif*, Kirk Street. A further set of lamps was obtained to make allowance for the three-year grace period but Provost MacGrory actually enjoyed the illuminations for a total of 12 years. He served two consecutive terms, thereby qualifying for nine years. His successor, Duncan McMillan, lived in a town centre flat and did not consider the erection of the Provost's lamps on the pavement of Longrow South to be entirely appropriate, so they remained in place at Kirk Street for a further three years.

Incidentally, one set of lamps still stands outside the Meadows Avenue home of Campbeltown's last Provost, Archie McCallum, where they are likely to remain for the foreseeable future. Another lamp is in the Campbeltown Heritage Centre and the Royal Burgh's twin town of Campbelltown, New South Wales, was presented with the remaining lamp some years ago.

Campbeltown's Provost, along with the two Bailies, automatically became Burgh Magistrates and took turns to sit on the bench of the old Burgh Court. Petty misdemeanours investigated by the police and brought to the attention of the Burgh Prosecutor found their way on to the court list, as opposed to the more serious cases dealt with at Campbeltown Sheriff Court.

As far back as my primary school days, I was amused by the local press coverage of the hearings, many of which were minor alcohol-related breaches of the peace with comical overtones. The names of certain characters cropped up with some regularity.

From the *Campbeltown Courier*, November 3 1960:

'A labourer who was drunk and incapable picked a convenient spot to collapse – outside the police station, Campbeltown Burgh Court was told on Monday. The man, J--- G--------, of – Street, Campbeltown, was fined £1 when he pleaded guilty by letter to a charge of being drunk and incapable.

'Bailie Ross said the man was not making a nuisance of himself. He was merely drunk, although he collapsed in a somewhat unusual place.'

October 30 1958: 'G----- T------- (21), and A-------- T------- (28), had a fight when they came into Campbeltown with their tinker families one Friday afternoon.

'The story was told at Campbeltown Burgh Court on Monday when they were each fined 10 shillings (50p).

'The Prosecutor said that some of the tinkers converged on the town for their usual drinking spree. Shortly before this offence occurred they were warned by the police to behave themselves but the two accused started fighting in Union Street and quite a crowd gathered. The police had to intervene.

'Bailie Anderson told the accused that if they had any differences to settle they should do it privately away in the country somewhere and not in the middle of the town.'

March 1962:

'A 34-year-old man led police and a group of citizens a merry chase after snatching three bottles of wine from a bicycle, Campbeltown Burgh Court was told on Monday.

'The Burgh Prosecutor said that three local men bought the wine and decided to go to a house to hold a celebration. Two of the men were walking down Union Street when the accused snatched the wine from a bicycle and ran. He was hotly pursued by the other two men down Union Street, across Longrow and up Burnside Street. Police later joined the chase and the accused was cornered in Harvey's Lane, where he dropped the wine bottles to the ground, smashing them.

'Provost A.P. MacGrory, presiding, fined P-----M-----, of ---------, £1 on the charge of stealing the wine and admonished him on a charge of depositing litter.'

A fine meted out fairly frequently was the standard five shillings (25p) punishment imposed on tenants who had suffered the misfortune of a domestic chimney fire, necessitating a visit by the fire brigade. Many other trivial matters such as illegal parking, cycling or parking without lights, and the discreetly worded charge of 'committing a nuisance' – urinating in a public place – were also dealt with by the Burgh Magistrates.

The Dean of Guild held an important position. This elected official and four other councillors formed the Dean of Guild Court, a very ancient institution.

Planning applications that were provisionally given the green light were endorsed only after a building warrant, guaranteeing certain safety conditions as laid down by law, had been issued. Building warrant applications laid before the Dean of Guild Court, therefore, would only be approved if the necessary criteria had been met.

The Court also had to listen to objections from parties affected by new building proposals and, ironically, this led to a full-blown Town Council row when the plans for Campbeltown's swimming pool came up for approval.

The site chosen by the Council bordered on a large privately owned villa set in extensive grounds and its owner objected to the plans. Despite the fact that the Dean of Guild Court in its entirety craved a swimming pool for the town, the decision was made that the objection was valid and the Council's application was turned down. The Town Hall chamber at the next full Council meeting was not a place for the faint-hearted!

The remaining councillor/official was the Burgh Treasurer and it was he who chaired the Finance Committee. It was also the Burgh Treasurer's duty to authorise any payments due by the Council to various parties and to liaise with the Burgh Chamberlain on the subject of the town's annual budget and setting of rates. Council

Tax, of course, was not even a figment in the most imaginative head and, if a few pennies were added to the burgh rates, the money was spent on Campbeltown and nowhere else.

Most Council business was discussed at the committee stage before being brought to the first available major meeting for approval or, alternatively, amendment.

A typical example of this function was a decision taken in February 1958, by the full Council to replace the Town Hall clock at a cost of £616:5s following proposals put forward by the Finance Committee. The various committees were: Housing; Housing Allocation; Quay and Harbour; Finance; Parks; Streets and Lighting; Entertainment; Public Health; and Library, which also included six members of the general public.

There were a number of regulars on the Council during my boyhood whose re-election chances were all but guaranteed.

John Anderson was, I suppose, the father of the Labour side of the chamber. A miner at the Argyll Colliery, he was known by his Christian name initials of JMB and served several terms, reaching the office of Bailie.

George McMillan first passed through the Town Hall portals as a young man in 1957 and served continuously until the Council's disbandment. He held various convenerships, became a Bailie, Provost, and it was a foregone conclusion that he would go on to represent Campbeltown on Strathclyde Regional Council before further reorganisation altered the boundary to embrace Argyll and Bute only. In all, George held office for a remarkable 42 years and is still a much-respected father figure in Campbeltown, serving on various important committees and initiative groups.

Other prominent Labour councillors were Duncan McMillan, Bill Stirling, Neil McCallum, William Campbell, Roger Gillespie and Alastair McKinlay, who currently sits as an Argyll and Bute Council member.

The *Progressive* and *Independent* banners were carried by councillors of a more right-wing inclination and were also well represented.

Archie McCallum, another current Argyll and Bute representative, was one of their number and he, too, rose through the ranks to become Provost of the town. George Halbert, one time manager of the local branch of the Clydesdale Bank, was another councillor who enjoyed ongoing success at the polls, as did Anthony MacGrory. Voters had continued confidence, also, in William Stevenson, a councillor from the age of 21 and a member to whom much credit was due for his part in organising the creation of Dalintober Beach. Daniel McKinven and William Craig, both of whom became Provosts, were two others who could count on generous support from the Campbeltown electors.

Before decanting to spacious new offices in a converted manse at Kirkland, Dell Road, the Council's paid officials were housed in a building which stood on the site of the present day Woolworth store at Old Quay Head. The municipal offices were reached by climbing an outside stairway on the building, which was demolished shortly after the officials moved around 1960.

The legal adviser to the Council was the Town Clerk, a qualified lawyer who additionally served as Clerk to the Burgh Court. A full-time post was created in 1956 to fill this role, the duties of which had previously been carried out by local solicitors on a part-time basis. The first Town Clerk to be appointed was a gentleman by the name of D.W.Anderson, though I cannot remember him at all. A further five Town Clerks held the position until 1966, three of whom I do recall seeing. They were Hugh Morton, John Kerr and Alan Matheson, who was also an excellent exponent of the bagpipes.

The Burgh Chamberlain's post was filled by an accountant and it was he who had the onerous task of setting the burgh rates on an annual basis, following consultation with the Finance Committee. Another of his responsibilities was as adviser to the Housing Allocation Committee over the letting of council houses, decided upon following scrutiny of the points system used for this purpose; a task that could be precarious at times! Bill Allan served as Campbeltown's Burgh Chamberlain for as long as I can remember.

The upkeep of the town's streets, pavements, paths, parks and public buildings was supervised by Burgh Surveyor David Kellock, who controlled a workforce comprising a burgh foreman and a team of manual council workmen. I seem to remember he had a penchant for granite chips when resurfacing work was done on the streets and coming off a bicycle unintentionally or scrabbling for pennies thrown at a wedding could be a painful experience. That being so, the disgraceful condition of some of Campbeltown's streets in early

2000 bears no comparison to the pothole-free roads enjoyed by motorists then.

The housing situation was high on the Council's priority list and a vigorous housebuilding programme was embarked upon in conjunction with the Scottish Special Housing Association. The Meadows and Calton estates were developed in the fifties and sixties to meet demand. And also, on May 30 1963, the Secretary of State for Scotland authorised Campbeltown Town Council to accept a tender of almost half a million pounds – submitted by Crudens Limited - for the construction of a further 199 houses on the Calton Redevelopment scheme to replace the ageing *prefabs*. Many other Council-owned properties were earmarked for renovation and by 1970 a total of 97.5% of all houses had been modernised.

'THE TWO MINUTES SILENCE'

The *Campbeltown Courier* is the only local newspaper to circulate in
the district, although in bygone days there were additional weeklies -
Argyllshire Herald and *Argyllshire Leader*- published in the town.
The paper's format for more than 100 years since its inception in
1873 was as a four-page, occasionally six, broadsheet, depending on
the amount of advertising copy.

As a former editor of the *Campbeltown Courier* - in the early 1970's
- I may well stand accused of being biased when I assert that the
weekly was a truly local newspaper of great character then and in the
preceding years. Granted, the well produced modern tabloid with
modern masthead and colour photographs is a credit to all
concerned, but the boundaries of the paper's true circulation area are
more often than not exceeded dramatically, especially now that the
title is incorporated with the *Argyllshire Advertiser*.

Since the newspaper was bought over from a Campbeltown family
concern by the group which also owns the *Oban Times* and
Argyllshire Advertiser, many news items are reported in the three
titles that are not strictly relevant to the area and the actual printing
of the *Courier* takes place at Falkirk, a long way from Campbeltown.
Announcements such as births, deaths and marriages and a certain
amount of advertising are also duplicated and I am often unable to
relate to people mentioned in these columns.

I have no wish to criticise the obviously profitable *Courier*, but
there are many non-local advertising features carried which, of
course, is good business, along with considerable number of general
pieces that really have little local bearing.

The *Campbeltown Courier* of February 18, 1960 carried an actual
404 column inches of genuinely local news out of possible 680
column inches. The remaining space was taken up by advertising of
a local nature.

The corresponding figures in the issue of February 19, 1999 fell a
long way short of these totals, though it was obvious that the 32-page
paper was a venture of real commercial success, and management
should be congratulated accordingly. A total of 3120 column inches
were available, out of which no less than 1730 inches were devoted

to local, duplicated and house advertising. Of the space left - 1390 column inches - only about 600,which included sports reports and 15 photographs, could be connected to the newspaper's generally recognised circulation area of Campbeltown, Kintyre, Gigha and Islay. Part of this total was a two-page splash on the thoughts of Argyll and Bute's four candidates for the forthcoming Scottish Parliament, an inordinate amount of space I would have thought. There were several articles on farming and motoring, more suited to trade publications, as well as articles on such diverse subjects as the Millennium Computer Bug and Credit Unions.

The next issue contained rather obscure articles on such topics as the advantages of using unleaded petrol, DVLA legislation, and news items from places as far afield as Inveraray, Lochgilphead and Craignish.

Campbeltonians of old knew the paper affectionately as *The Two Minutes Silence*. As with all small local newspapers, however, it was eagerly snapped up every Thursday morning and many copies were sent to exiles in all corners of the globe either by the front shop assistants or relatives in the town.

The editorial staff consisted of an editor and reporter, both of whom shared an equal workload in the gathering of the week's news. The printing room was manned, variously, by a workforce of four or five men who operated linotype machines and handset the paper's headlines. Most of the town's commercial printing orders were also dealt with here.

Well-known printers in the fifties and sixties era were Willie McLeod, Bob Albyn, Denis MacKay, Billy Ralston, Hamish McIntyre, Dennis Penman and Wellwood McMartin.

Two young local reporters of the period went on to become respected names in Scottish journalism. Malcolm Speed progressed to the coveted editor's chair of the *Daily Record* and John McKinlay completed his career as assistant news editor on *The Herald*.

The issue of March 10, 1960, was the first to come off a new flatbed-printing machine that was bought in Otley, Yorkshire. The 400-mile journey by lorry was not without incident when the truck ran into a heavy snowstorm and was stranded for 24 hours in a deep drift, a mere three miles from Campbeltown.

The publication of photographs was a drawn-out affair, which involved the photographer, British European Airways and a Glasgow printing block firm. Processed black and white pictures were sent by air on the scheduled daily Glasgow flight from Machrihanish Airport and collected at Abbotsinch – the former name of Glasgow International Airport – by a representative of John Swain and Son, York Street. When the necessary metal engraving process required then for newspaper reproduction was complete, Swains returned the blocks on the next available flight.

The readers' letters column also seemed more interesting, even controversial, than now and there were several regular correspondents whose views were sure to raise comment. Denis MacKay senior, father of the aforementioned printer, and local shopkeeper Jack McKinven, a gentleman with an apparently unending store of colourful words and phrases, were two oft-quoted scribes. A man called Muir wrote regularly from distant Canada using the pseudonym of *Tillicum* and George Meachan, exiled in darkest Corby, seldom missed an opportunity to air his views on topical matters relating to his native burgh.

Cartoons, a number of which were drawn in his spare time by talented local upholsterer Dan Kerr, appeared regularly. I recall one in particular that was published shortly after the announcement that the American military was sending a detachment to RAF Machrihanish. Depicted were two old Guernsey-clad, pipe-smoking Campbeltown fishermen standing at the head of the Old Quay - surrounded by uniformed, cigar-smoking, camera-toting GI's. The caption read: 'Did ye' hear the Yanks wis comin' Wullie'?

Looking through the advertising columns of former issues of the *Campbeltown Courier* brings memories of long obsolete products flooding back. In the paper of January 13, 1955, an advertisement extolling the virtues of a new television set placed by John Shields, Radio and Cycle Agent, 70 Longrow, proudly proclaimed: 'First in Britain. The KB Turret Tuner. 17-inch screen. 88 guineas (£92:40p). KB again lead in technical design with Britain's first Turret Tuner in this handsome model that will receive every possible future programme – BBC or Commercial.' Did that earnest claim include satellite and digital television, I wonder?

The local garages advertised new and used cars with delightfully evocative names including Humber Hawk; Standard Vanguard; Hillman Minx; Austin Somerset; Morris Isis; Ford Zephyr; Vauxhall Velox; Rover Ninety; Singer Gazelle.

In July 1961, Duncan Ramsay's garage offered a brand new Ford Consul Classic for £744:17:6d, inclusive of Purchase Tax, which was an early form of VAT.

The SCWS advertised its food lines extensively, especially items such as tea, sugar and flour. Whisky was also heavily featured.

I have chronicled a random selection of extracts from news stories of a diverse nature taken from the columns of the *Campbeltown Courier* which, I hope, gives some indication of local life as it was in the fifties and sixties.

DECEMBER 2, 1954: 'Last Friday evening the Dail-an-Tobhair Junior Choir, under their conductor, Miss Isa Graham, provided their own townsfolk with a demonstration of the quality of the singing which won them the coveted Rona MacVicar Trophy at this year's National Mod. They sustained a two and a half-hour programme without noticeably tiring for their voices were as fresh and true at the end of the evening as at the beginning. It was a superb performance and the only criticism which might be made is that the young soloists would have done well enough singing just one song instead of two and so allowed a little more time for group and choral items.

One of the highlights of the evening was the vigorous singing of the boys' ensemble.

'Gus McAllister's band, who supplied the music for an enjoyable dance which followed later, also played a lively selection of Scottish airs midway through the programme and contributed to the real ceilidh spirit which made this a most invigorating evening.'

APRIL 7, 1955: 'The opening of the new clothing factory yesterday, a branch of the firm of Messrs Andrew Douglas Ltd., by the Earl of Home, Minister of State for Scotland, marked the culmination of, and set the seal upon, the high hopes of the townsfolk for the successful outcome of the most promising development of local industry in this century.

'Anyone who knew the Albyn Distillery in The Roading, at Millknowe, particularly the interior, would hardly recognise it now as is shown in our picture of the building as it appears today. The transformation began in the autumn of 1953 when Mr Bannatyne, manager of the Campbeltown Employment Exchange, pressed the claims of Campbeltown as a suitable site for a light industry with his Ministry of Labour headquarters.

'The firm of Messrs Andrew Douglas Ltd. were at that time looking for premises for a new branch and were then actually negotiating for the purchase of a factory in the Borders. They became interested in Campbeltown as an alternative but Mr. Bannatyne was determined to 'sell' them the idea.'

SEPTEMBER 8, 1955: 'Mr. William Armour, 19 Glentorran Place, Campbeltown's last surviving coppersmith, died on Sunday in his 78th year.

'Mr. Armour had served a lifetime in the trade with the firm of Robert Armour and Sons. He started with the firm as an apprentice in the shop at the age of 15.

'About 40 years ago Mr. Armour took a prominent part in the organisation of the annual trades processions in which the various trades of the town were represented on lorry tableaux. Mr. Armour's own lorry always had s shining copper model of a still incorporated in the general design.'

AUGUST 14, 1958: 'Thousands of people lined Campbeltown's streets under grey skies on Monday evening to welcome their Queen. If the weather lacked sunshine, the welcome certainly did not.

'Every man, women and child for miles around turned out to pay their loyal tribute. It was a welcome the town will remember with pride for many a year. And luckily the rain stayed away – until the very last minute. Just as the Queen was stepping into the Royal barge at the end of her 45-minute visit, the clouds opened and the rain came down in a cloudburst.

'After the presentations Campbeltown Gaelic Choir under their conductor, Mr. M. G. McCallum, sang four songs. The last was 'God Bless the Prince of Wales.' The Queen and Duke smiled at each other in surprise. They nodded their approval as the kilted singers sang their tribute to Prince Charles, recently ordained Prince of Wales.

'Dozens of small craft took people out from the harbour to sail round Britannia but conditions were so bad that little activity could be seen aboard the yacht.

'Local Boy Scouts added their own contribution. They climbed up Summerhill to illuminate their huge ER sign.

'The boys had collected nearly 200 old paint tins and filled them with waste. At 10 o'clock they soaked them with oil and ignited the cans.'

'Much of the space in this 'Courier' was given over to coverage of the Royal visit and the following week's paper was a special souvenir issue.

JANUARY 7, 1960: 'Archie Nimmo, the former Campbeltown Grammar schoolboy had his big moment at Cathkin Park on Saturday when he scored the winning goal in his senior football debut.

'Archie, playing at centre for Partick Thistle, was one of the team's successes in the game against Third Lanark.

'Archie went straight to Firhill from school, signing on a professional form that summer. He played several trials for Clyde before Thistle became interested.

'Manager Willie Thornton must be pleased with Archie's first showing and fans say he is one of the best prospects they have seen at Firhill for a long time.

'Archie's family live at Drumlemble.'

SEPTEMBER 1, 1960: 'The fire at Argyll Colliery, Machrihanish, is out. A National Coal Board spokesman told the 'Courier' that by the middle of last week, the samples that were being taken every three hours indicated that the gases given off by combustion were no longer present.

'The Mine Rescue Brigade crews from Coatbridge have returned to their depot and production is being resumed on a limited scale in a section near the pit bottom.

'The fire had lasted about 12 days and had led to the colliery's labour force of almost 200 receiving notice of redundancy. Our reporter understands that the redundancy notices have been withdrawn and there will be no cut in the number of workers.'

SEPTEMBER 22, 1960: 'This has been a memorable year for a 26-year-old Kintyre shepherd, who has won fame for Campbeltown by his skill as a drum-major. He has already defeated the world champion drum major and is being hailed as his successor.

'But despite his successes, Ian Lang is still the same modest young man he was always been. Though proud of his competition awards, he always puts his band first, and is almost shy of publicity.

'But on Saturday, Ian, of Princes Street, Campbeltown, is to be honoured by his town. The Town Council Entertainment Committee is to make a presentation to him at the closing ceremony of its summer activities in Kilkerran Green on Saturday evening.

'He was Cowal Games champion last year and in the past 12 months has won drum majors' competitions at Edinburgh, Rothesay and Greenock. A few weeks ago Ian led the massed bands at the Cowal Games.'

OCTOBER 27, 1960: 'Campbeltown's oldest industry, the networks in Kinloch Road, is busier than ever. Indeed, to cope with orders, its premises are stretched to capacity. That is why the networks owners, Joseph Gundry and Co. Ltd., are putting up buildings which will increase the floor space by more than a third.

'The new buildings are a rigging shed, where nets are made up and mounted to ropes and a driving shed, in which nets that have been tarred or barked to aid preservation are dried off.

'The town's oldest industry is certainly one of the most progressive. Apart from the infinite variety of nets which are made not only in the traditional cotton but in the new man-made fibres, nylon and courlene, orders come from all over the world – from Canada, Africa and Iceland, as well as from Scotland and Ireland.

'The factory is probably one of the most deceptive in the whole of the West of Scotland. Its unimposing façade in Kinloch Road suggests a small warehouse, with an equally small weaving shed. But, once inside, one almost gets lost as one moves from department to department.

'Campbeltown's networks, which was established more than 100 years ago as Thomas Brown and Co., is now part of an even older firm – Joseph Gundry and Co. Ltd. established their Bridport factory almost 300 years ago – but the manager is a Campbeltown man, Councillor Hugh Norman. He has been the architect of much of the factory's progress in recent years.

'He is to be congratulated in helping to keep alive a traditional craft of his native town.'

JULY 13, 1961: 'A proposal that Campbeltown Town Council should limit the number attending Saturday night dances in the Victoria Hall to 600 was rejected by the Council at its monthly meeting on Monday.

'Councillor William Stirling, who said that he did not think the Council should allow any more than 600 in the hall, made the proposal. He had been informed by one of the hall attendants the previous Saturday that a crowd of more than 600 was just too much for attendants to handle.

'The proposal was seconded by Bailie S.A.Ross, who said that, in addition to the question of a fire risk, the ventilation in the hall was most inadequate.

'Dean of Guild Dan McKinven, who said the Council should take no action to limit the number of dancers, claimed that a restriction in numbers was not the answer to the problem of making dances comfortable or enjoyable. The answer was to limit admission in terms of the condition of would-be dancers.

'Supporting the Dean of Guild, Councillor Hugh Norman said he felt the Council was developing an awful habit of putting on petty restrictions that served no useful purpose and only impaired the enjoyment of the public.

'The Council rejected the proposal by nine votes to seven.'

FEBRUARY 14, 1963: ' It was only at the weekend that Kintyre returned to something like normal after the three days of isolation following the blizzards which hit Scotland on Tuesday and Wednesday.

'The toll, in terms of damage to property, was surprisingly light. Remarkably, too, there were no reports of death or injury among the population; but sheep farmers sustained heavy losses and hundreds of dead sheep were dug out of deep snowdrifts.

'One of this worst hit communities was Southend. The village was cut off for four days and for three of these was deprived of electricity. Telephone subscribers were also cut off.

'In Campbeltown, burgh workmen worked until midnight on Wednesday and Thursday evenings, clearing snow from Longrow and Main Street, with the aid of bulldozers and lorries. But with the glaring lack of equipment in Kintyre to deal with the exceptional conditions, the picture on road communications was indeed grim. Fortunately, private citizens and private and public industrial concerns showed plenty of initiative. The Machrihanish road was reopened on Friday afternoon, thanks to the efforts of men and machines from Argyll Colliery, helped by County roadmen from Drumlemble and men from Stewarton village.

'On Friday, with stocks of flour and bread beginning to run low, a fishing boat was chartered by the Post Office to take mail and stranded businessmen from Campbeltown to Tarbert to catch the Gourock mail steamer, *Lochfyne*. The boat brought back incoming mail that had accumulated at Tarbert along with more than 3000 loaves, vegetables, flour and other foodstuffs. The fishing boat, the *Star of Hope* (CN 149) also brought in the first national newspapers to reach the town in three days.'

APRIL 8, 1965: 'Campbeltown's dustmen have adopted an unusual and distinctive uniform – a bowler hat.

'Last week householders in the town watched with amazement as the friendly dustmen in their new headdress called to collect the refuse. And, everywhere they went crowds of excited and curious children gathered round.

'The burgh's scavenging men claim it is all part of their contribution towards boosting the town's tourist industry.

'Two leading members of the 'bowler brigade' – Mr. Peter Robertson (53), of 4 Fisher Row, and 39-year-old Mr. Ernest Mitchell, of 169 Ralston Road – spoke on Friday of how they got the idea.

'Said Mr. Mitchell: "During our collections last Friday we found the hats among rubbish dumped by tenants of the flats at 53 Longrow. Just for a laugh, we wore them all that day."

'Mr. Robertson explained: " After that people began to ask us where they were so we put them back on on Monday."

'Footnote: The bowler hats were thrown out by Mrs. David Scally during her spring-cleaning. Said Mrs. Scally: "I don't mind what the dustmen do with the hats. It is really very funny."'

'DOON THE QUAY'

Campbeltown Harbour, which comprises the Old Quay, New Quay and the Dalintober anchorage, is rightly regarded as being among the safest and most easily accessed on the West Coast of Scotland. Commercially however, this haven which one sheltered a mighty fishing fleet and many merchant and naval vessels now presents but a ghostly image of its illustrious past.

It is true to say, though, that the structural condition of both quays is excellent - thanks to considerable public expenditure - and the whole area gives an agreeable impression of a well-maintained harbour, due in no small measure to the indefatigable William McDonald, Harbour Master.

The construction of a linkspan and terminal building on the New Quay, created to accommodate the needs of the Argyll and Antrim Steam Packet Company's Campbeltown-Ballycastle car ferry, is also a valuable asset. Unfortunately, after only three loss-making short summer seasons, the company has reconsidered its options and the future of the service is doubtful, despite efforts by certain parties to reopen the run. People on both sides of the North Channel have pointed the finger at poor marketing as the root cause of the trouble but, Irish ferry or not, many local people feel that much more use can be made of the costly berthing facility that lies dormant for the greater part of the year.

Some idea of the bustle that was Campbeltown Harbour of my youth can be obtained by referral to the details of harbour dues collected from various visiting vessels - fishing boats excluded – during the month of December, 1957.

This four-week period saw a total of £608:14s: 3d paid over by an impressive 53 vessels, two of which were HM ships. In addition to the provision of berthing manpower, 20400 gallons of fresh water were supplied to ships by the Campbeltown Harbour authorities. More than 35000 gallons of whisky were imported, with 10556 gallons exported. Almost 750 tons of coal came ashore at Campbeltown and a substantial 13285 tons from the Argyll Colliery were exported. Other imports were tarred road metals (397 tons); cattle feed (105 tons); oil (128 tons).

Sea transport around the Scottish west coast and islands was still a vital part of daily life and a wide variety of commodities were brought in by boat, including coal, bricks, lime, building sand, whisky, grain, timber, oil and so on. The vessels used for carrying the goods were of the *puffer* type, so called because of the ever-present pall of black funnel smoke caused by the coal burning engineroom furnace that heated the boiler. Puffers were commonplace at the various commercial berths in Campbeltown Harbour and their personnel became well known in the shops and pubs of the town. It is easy to recall the vessels' names that sailed under the flags of companies such as Ross and Marshall, Hay and Hamilton and I shall mention a few here: *Stormlight; Raylight; Lady Isle; Dawnlight; Limelight; Glen Cloy;Glen Rosa; Glen Shira; Spartan; Pibroch; Kaffir; Moonlight; Invercloy.* I can also remember the *Halcyon*, a vessel that regularly visited her home port, having been owned by a Campbeltown man, Mr. William McMillan. For some reason this vessel, with her large counter stern, reminded me of a Chinese Junk, such was her unusual design.

As can be seen from the harbour dues figures, coal from the Argyll Colliery at Machrihanish was shipped from Campbeltown in some considerable quantity. Most of the coal, which was perhaps better utilised in industrial furnaces rather than domestic fires, was exported to Ulster for use in Kilroot Power Station. The vessels that carried the black diamonds were known as the Kelly Boats and three regular visitors were the *Ballylumford, Ballyrobert* and *Ballykelly.* They were much larger than the Clyde puffers, having been designed to stand up to the foul weather conditions experienced during the winter months in the North Channel.

The coal boats were loaded by a simple but effective method at a berth directly opposite the site of the present-day diesel oil storage tank on the north side of the Old Quay. NCB lorries from the colliery tipped their loads into a cavernous hopper on the quay. From this hopper a stoutly ridged conveyor belt carried the coal upward to a big swivel-headed spout that could be directed to any part of the ship's hold. The angle of the conveyor belt casing and the spout could be altered to suit any state of the tide.

Some of the vessels carried 1000 tons of coal and two were often seen in Campbeltown on the same day.

The NCB lorries that ran the coal from Machrihanish were mainly six-wheeled Leyland Hippo tippers. The drivers were greatly attached to their vehicles and some even had individual nameplates - fashioned by the pit engineers on the quiet - affixed to the bodywork Hippo club members were Angus Morrison (*Ceannloch*), Jim Coffield, Donald McCallum, Hugh Anderson and John Halliday. Willie McSporran drove a Dennis Jubilant named *Loch Fyne*, Dan Girvan had a Seddon and Alec Mason undertook coal deliveries to miners' homes in a smaller Albion drop-side lorry.

Each driver completed 11 runs per day, amounting to 110 miles, from the pit to the Old Quay when the coal boats were in port. I spent many an enjoyable hour during school holidays in the cab of Angus Morrison's *Ceannloch*, with his son Jackie, as the lorry growled its way back and forth.

Nowadays, it is an event to see a merchant ship in Campbeltown, the only occasional visitors being timber carriers to load with felled coniferous trees.

The Campbeltown fishing fleet has also contracted steadily over the years and currently only 12 inshore vessels, mainly small prawn trawlers, are based at the Old Quay. As most boats carry two men only, the number of fishermen sailing from the town has reached an all-time low of around 30. It is difficult to comprehend that, little more than 100 years ago, the incredible total of 2080 herring fishermen sailed from Campbeltown in a fleet of 604 sailing skiffs. Heady days indeed, but hark back to the more recent 1950's, when Campbeltown could boast a magnificent fleet of modern herring ring net vessels that was one of the finest in the country. The serried ranks of ringers, each one in pristine condition, took up most of the berthing space in the inner harbour – the traditional territory of the herring men.

Although the boats have now all gone, their magical names are still remembered and spoken of sentimentally in Campbeltown. The following list comes from a CN register of fishing vessels with a gross tonnage in excess of 15 - including several from neighbouring Carradale - during the early fifties.

Florian (CN 2)
Water Cress (CN 3)

Elma (CN 25)
Westering Home (CN 26)
Moira (CN 33)
Nobles Again (CN 37)
Irma (CN 45)
Almanzora (CN 54)
Acacia (CN 56)
Seafarer (CN 77)
Janet Lang (CN 84)
Kestrel (CN 93)
Kittiwake (CN 94)
Falcon (CN 97)
Nan MacMurrar (CN 105)
Escallonia (CN 110)
Marion 2 (CN 111)
Margaret Rose (CN 115)
Marie Elspeth (CN 116)
Regina Maris (CN 118)
Golden Dawn (CN 119)
Lily Oak (CN 131)
Endeavour (CN 132)
Boy Danny (CN 142)
Amalthea (CN 143)
Stella Maris (CN 158)
Anne Philomena (CN 159)
Rhu-na-Gal (CN 163)
Kathleen (CN 164)
Fiona (CN 165)
Harvest Queen (CN 167)
Golden Fleece (CN 170)
Maid of Morven (CN 177)
Annie (CN 178)
Morag Bhan (CN 183)
Margaret Newton (CN 184)
Maureen (CN 185)
Elizabeth Campbell (CN 186)
Mary McLean (CN 193)
Jessie (CN 194)
Jessie MacKinnon (CN 196)

Florentine (CN 197)
Golden Hind (CN 199)
Bengullion (CN 229)
Nobles (CN 236)
Felicia (CN 237)
May (CN 243)
Amy Harris (CN 249)
Glen Carradale (CN 253)
Mairi Bhan (CN 259)
Kingbird (CN 264)
Queen of the Fleet (CN 269)

Monday mornings were a hive of activity at the Old Quay as the ring
net fleet prepared for the toil ahead. The boats worked from sunset
until sunrise, including Friday nights, and the crews rested during the
day.

Provisions for the week had to be stowed away and bags of coal, a
very necessary commodity that stoked the forecastle stove during the
long cold nights, were barrowed to each boat by its cook - a position
normally held by the most junior crewman. Road tankers delivered
the diesel fuel needed to drive engines bearing such distinguished
names as Kelvin, Gardner, Gleniffer and McLaren. A familiar sight
then was the old red-painted wagon which belonged to Murdoch
Weir, and its asthmatic progress from his Kinloch Road depot could
easily be noted by the accompanying plume of blue-grey exhaust
fumes that rose high in the air on quiet mornings. Murdoch also
supplied a range of ship chandlery to the boats.

Occasionally, the cotton-twined herring ring net had to be treated
with preservative and this was another Monday morning chore
carried out at the nearby Joseph Gundry net factory. It was an
operation not exactly eagerly anticipated by fishermen as it involved
a smelly, dirty process known as *barking* - using a tar based liquid
with a decidedly pungent odour - and was definitely a case for
wearing the oldest clothes available.

When the herring fleet made its annual winter pilgrimage to *The
North*, fishing the grounds of the Outer Hebrides from bases in
Castlebay, Barra, and Lochboisdale, South Uist, preparations were
made on a grander scale and massive flat net barrows were used to
transport substantial amounts of *dry* stores to the quayside. It was not

unknown for the boats to be laid up at anchor by bad weather for anything up to a week in remote bights or lochs and a good supply of emergency rations was vital to sustain the crews during the gales. The ringers also made long seasonal treks to the popular tourist resorts of Whitby, on the Yorkshire coast and the Isle of Man, both of which were enjoyed immensely by the younger fishermen.

Real pride was taken in the vessels and the majority had varnished hulls and wheelhouses. The traditionally slack herring fishing period in late spring and early summer saw the boats laid up for the annual *cleaning* operation, which could last for six weeks. Most of the boats had special supporting legs fitted to let the hull stand upright on the beach when the tide receded, thus allowing access to all areas of the lower planking, keel, propeller and rudder for maintenance and anti-fouling treatment. The favoured beaching site was along the Hall Street sea wall that separates the Old and New Quays, anchored bows-in to permit as many vessels as possible to make use of the facility.

Each skipper wanted his boat to look the best at the end of the beaching period and friendly rivalry prevailed among the fishermen as the meticulous work progressed. Viewing the results of their labours afterwards on a sunny morning was a pleasure to the eye, when the hulls positively glistened in the calm, shimmering harbour seawater - the tiny ripples creating multi-patterned dancing reflections on the new varnish or paintwork.

A few weeks later, during the holiday season when the boats still looked their immaculate best, a harbour regatta was held. As part of Campbeltown's Civic Week, this gala occasion included a fishing boat race when the vessels, bedecked with bunting and loaded with spectators, steamed out from the Old Quay to the Millbeg Buoy and back. Indeed, it was at the regatta of 1958 that I began my life-long love affair with fishing boats when I boarded the 55-foot ring netter, *Moira (CN 33)*, and took to the high seas on such a vessel for the first time. The Ceannloch Pipe Band sometimes played on the deck of a fishing boat in the inner harbour, where all kinds of watersports, my favourite being the *greasy pole*, took place. One year I saw a man simultaneously water-skiing and playing the bagpipes, and another, tightly secured inside a huge sack, being thrown into the water to enthral us with a daring act of escapology.

Most of the ring net skippers have since passed on, but many, like me, will remember some of the stalwarts who pursued the method almost until the bitter end. It has been maintained that the demise of the fishery was partly brought about by the introduction of destructive pair trawling by huge powerful vessels from the Scottish East Coast and Northern Ireland.

Herring ringing involved two purpose built boats of 50-odd feet, known locally as *neebours*, and some of the eminent Campbeltown pairs in the early sixties were: *Stella Maris* and *Regina Maris* (skippers Jim Meenan and Pat MacKay); *Nobles Again* and *Moira* (skippers Tommy Ralston and Neil Speed); *Golden Hind* and *Boy Danny* (skippers Duncan McDonald and Willie Stewart); *Fiona* and *Mary McLean* (skippers Peter McKinlay and Duncan McArthur); *Star of Hope* and *Harvest Hope* (skippers Malcolm McGougan and James McDonald). Of the above, only Duncan McArthur and James McDonald are still with us.

The north side of the Old Quay was unofficially reserved for the smaller seine-netters and creel boats. The development of the seine-net method and the large number of visiting boats led to substantial white fish landings at Campbeltown. This situation filled a void since the Clyde herring landing ports had been designated as Ayr and Tarbert. Some of the local fishermen who switched successfully to white fish catching - i.e. cod, haddock, whiting, plaice etc - were James Wareham (*Jessie CN 194*); Neil Lang (*Janet Lang CN 84*); Robbie McKellar (*Golden Chance CN 18*); Cecil Finn (*Brighter Morn CN 151*); Jim McLean (*Sea Nymph CN 70*); John Robertson (*Felicity- CN 64*); John Short (*Florian CN 2*). Skipper Finn progressed to become one of the West Coast's top fishermen and, ultimately, President of the Scottish Fishermen's Federation. He was awarded both the MBE and OBE for his services to the industry.

A mini-fleet of trim little Scottish Northeast Coast white fish seine-netters – *forty-fitters* as they were known - used Campbeltown as a seasonal base. Ports such as Whitehills, Portnockie, Cullen, Banff and Peterhead were represented and a few names which come to mind are *Prosperity; Harvest Gleaner; Loyalty; Ocean Harvester; Ha'burn; Avail; Green Pastures; Devotion; Sincerity; Dulcie*. During the winter and spring months, when fair weather permitted, the Old Quay on most weekday evenings bustled with frenetic endeavour as the various buyers vied with one another in an attempt to meet their bosses' stipulated requirements. Lorries belonging to Harvey Giffen, West Coast Motors and British Road Services were piled high with the old style wooden fish boxes by fish lumpers – men who usually had a day job but took the opportunity to earn extra cash on a casual labour basis.

The repartee between the various buyers at the fish auctions was, to say the least, educational to my young ears and could also be uproariously funny at times. Where have the larger than life characters like John (*Latcher*) Durnan, Malcolm (*Mucka*) McMillan, John (*Jock Ock*) McIntyre and Archie (*Smeesh*) Smith gone? A later and, indeed, important buyer to the local fleet was Tommy (*Tucker*) Robertson, whose off the cuff witticisms were the source of much hilarity at the Old Quay. Add local fishmongers Donnie Gilchrist and Jimmy Thomson and the entertainment was complete.

The New Quay provided moorings for frequent visits by Royal Navy warships and submarines. It was home, also, to the RNLI 52-foot Barnett Class lifeboat *City of Glasgow 2*, which lay in constant readiness on a Mediterranean Moor. Commissioned in 1953, the lifeboat responded successfully to many maritime Mayday calls under the coxswainship of the celebrated Duncan Newlands and his successor Archie Malcolm.

Many other vessels and small craft, of course, used the harbour. The famous Clyde steamer *doon the watter* trips were still very much in vogue and Campbeltown was the outward extremity of certain excursions. Regular visitors to the town were the Caledonian Steam Packet Company vessels *Duchess of Hamilton* and *Duchess of Montrose*, two graceful steam turbine ships with a good turn of speed. In addition, the paddle steamers *Waverley* and *Caledonia* berthed often at Campbeltown.

Music, generally of Scottish country dance band origin, blared from crackling speakers mounted on the Old Quay harbour buildings – which stood on the site of the present-day fish market – as the steamers approached, and continued throughout the afternoon. When the passenger boats came alongside, big iron gates cordoned off part of the Old Quay and there were three sets of turnstiles through which travellers had to pass to gain access to the gangways at a cost of one old penny. The turnstiles were enclosed in little hut like structures, sometimes manned on a part time basis by crusty old pensioners. Occasionally, a fishing boat would be moored with her bow section on one side of the dividing line and her stern on the other, and it was our sheer delight as youngsters to sneak on board the boat, walk its length and gain free access to the forbidden territory - to the extreme annoyance of the aged gentlemen.

A common summer sound at around 3.55pm in the Royal Burgh was the eerie drone of the steamers' foghorns, which were always set off to warn of the vessels' impending departure. Many an agitated figure could be seen running down the Old Quay at the last minute, fearful of missing the boat - the lateness caused perhaps by additional socialising after the pubs closed at 2.30pm.

Campbeltown was also used as a base by the Scottish Fisheries Protection vessel, *Rona*, in the days when an archaic law – thankfully long since repealed - prevented small inshore boats from using an otter trawl inside the three-mile limit. The Leith-registered *Rona* was an old vessel of some 100 feet in length and was the butt of many a joke. Nicknamed *The Cutter*, her presence could be detected at a great distance by the black reek of her funnel. Speed was not one of her attributes, either, and one Campbeltown boat, the *Golden Hind*, could actually outrun her. She did, nevertheless, successfully snare a few unsuspecting skippers in her time.

A popular harbour activity in summer was the hiring of rowing dinghies and little inboard motor boats. Bertie Craig, whose son, Alec, now runs a coal business in Campbeltown, had a 24-strong flotilla of small varnished craft, previously owned by James O'Hara, which could be boarded at the New Quay slipway. The Stuart Turner-powered motor boats were pure magnetism to small boys such as myself and, if a state of affluence prevailed, the rowing dinghies took a very definite second place. The Craigs also owned two larger white painted clinker-built launches, *Morning Star* and *Evening Star*, and they were used under the auspices of Archie McGougan to carry passengers to Davaar Island and the famous Cave Picture – a depiction of the Crucifixion painted on a cave wall in the 1880's by local artist Archibald MacKinnon. Duncan Newlands also ran to the island in a big varnished carvel launch called the *May Allan*. This manifestly valuable tourism asset has, regrettably, never been developed to its full potential.

Another hirer was John Shields, who constructed a unique floating roundabout for kiddies that included fibreglass model liners, submarines and seabirds. The structure was powered by a Seagull outboard motor and brought joy to many youngsters. John also hired out kayaks at Dalintober Beach.

No reference to the Campbeltown Harbour of bygone days would be complete without mentioning the little burgundy-painted building that stood for so many years at the head of the Old Quay, on the seaward side of the Cross. This was the town's weighhouse, incorporating a weighbridge, where the tonnage of shipping cargo was recorded. Known locally as *The Wee Uss*, its walls were more often than not surrounded by off-duty fishermen and streetwise philosophers indulging in the yarns of the day. It was a favourite gathering place and its demolition to make away for the development of a traffic roundabout was tinged with sadness for many.

EMPLOYMENT

Campbeltown, unfortunately, entered the Millennium and its coincidental tercentenary with the unenviable distinction of being one of Scotland's worst unemployment blackspots.
The run-down of the fishing industry, whisky distilling and blending, closures of Argyll Colliery, Gundry's Networks, Campbeltown Shipyard, building firms and the mothballing of RAF Machrihanish have all gradually contributed to the serious loss of job opportunities that has created a consequent adverse knock on effect on the local economy. The latest kick in the teeth occurred shortly before Christmas 1999, when model aeroplane makers, K.V.Wooster, announced its closure with the resultant loss of 40 vital jobs.
Looking back to the period under discussion, though, I cannot recall any widespread feeling of pessimism, young as I was. It was certainly no ideal world but generally speaking as far as I can remember, there was work of some kind available for most people who sought it. A recent conversation I had on Gigha with another Campbeltown expatriate, John Martin, bears this out when he recalled wistfully that on leaving Campbeltown Grammar School in 1956, he had the choice of three different apprenticeships before deciding to become a joiner in Malcolm Martin's Glebe Street workshop.
The National Coal Board was an important employer, with an underground workforce of 200 miners at the Argyll Colliery. There were also management and office staff, engineers, lorry drivers and other surface workers at the pit.
Although the herring fishing industry suffered a slump as the 1950's wore on, a considerable number of fishermen still sailed
from the port on board both herring and white fish boats and the development of the prawn and scallop fisheries was just around the corner. Allied to the fishing industry, of course, was another significant place of employment, the Joseph Gundry Networks in Kinloch Road, which had a mixed male and female labour team.
Astonishingly, there were 34 distilleries producing whisky in Campbeltown at one time. By the 1950's, however, only two remained – Springbank (presently employing 27) and Glen Scotia -,

both of which are still in operation. A number of jobs were available on the production side and also for coopers and warehousemen, since there were still bonded warehouses at Glebe Street, Lochend and Hazleburn.

The retailing side of the local commercial set-up was also a source of work for a lot of people. Around 120 men and women were employed in the grocery trade, and a further 80 had jobs with the bakers and butchers; David Kerr's butcher shop in Main Street alone had a staff of 16. The remainder of the retailers accounted for many jobs, especially when one considers, for instance, that the four large furniture stores also employed men as undertakers and upholsterers. It has been estimated that the six garages employed around 70 mechanics, salesmen and office staff. Two notable car salesmen of the era were Russell Knox at the County Garage and Lamont Conley, of Neil Paterson Ltd.

There were, of course, considerably more qualified tradesmen at work in Campbeltown than now. One of the main companies was Robert Weir and Son, who employed up to 60 men as joiners, bricklayers, slaters and plasterers. The building firm of Ferguson and the joinery business of Malcolm Martin eventually joined forces with Weir to become a consortium known as WFM. Lack of work as the years have progressed, though, has caused the company's closure, with unavoidable redundancies.

It was about this time that the Kintyre Farmers co-operative was formed and its Glebe Street headquarters recruited tradesmen such as electricians, plumbers and joiners. The KF also had an egg packing station and animal feed store at Glebe Street.

Some of the other *trades* concerns that spring to mind include Neil McArthur, builders; Henry McGougan, builders; McKinlay and Blair, electricians; James Stott, builders; J.McLachlan, joiners and coachbuilders; McShannon and Duncan, painters; J.and M.McDougall, coachbuilders; John McDougall, joiners; Robert Armour and Sons, plumbers; W.G.Prosser, slaters and plasterers; Murray and Gillies, electricians; D.McKillop, painters; Malcolm Lang, plumbers; James Grant, electricians; R.Wilkie, joiners; Campbeltown Sawmill, joiners; Galbraith and Cochrane, painters;Thomas McPherson, slaters; Charles McSporran, engineers; Hamilton Brothers, engineers; Duncan McQuilkan, electricians; J.Garbutt, painters; MacFarlane-Shearer, animal feed suppliers.

Transport in and around Campbeltown and further afield also provided a good number of jobs, allowing for the fact that the British Road Services fleet based at the Kinloch Road depot consisted of some 30 lorries. There were several smaller transport outfits and the two bus companies, West Coast Motors and A. &P.McConnachie, employed a number of mechanics as well as drivers and conductresses.

White-collar work was available in the various area offices of the old Argyll County Council, which accounted for 70 jobs, the Municipal Offices at Dell Road and in a number of other professional premises in town.

Both the Royal Mail and Telephone Exchange sections of the GPO were well staffed. The modern BT technicians' squad is small in comparison to the number - estimated at around 45 - of GPO engineers, linesmen and telephonists previously employed in Campbeltown.

The Scottish Gas Board had a workforce of 40, compared to the present five, and the North of Scotland Hydro Electric Board's roll also exceeded its present counterpart's total by a long way.

I suppose technological developments over the years have led to the inevitable trimming of manpower. Campbeltown's gas supply, for example, was made in the town's gasworks at the top of Glebe Street from coal carried to the Old Quay by cargo boats. Nowadays, road tankers deliver the natural gas in liquified form and it is held in storage tanks on the site of the old Millknowe School before being easily converted when required to meet consumer demand.

One job carried out then by Gas Board workmen always intrigued me and it is only now that I have discovered what it was all about. There was a drain cover in Ralston Road, just past the rear entrance to the Grammar School, and, at regular intervals, a gasman would appear on a bicycle with a portable brass stirrup pump slung over his shoulder. When the cover was lifted and the apparatus duly assembled, vigorous pumping produced a spurt of brown smelly water that ran into a nearby sewer. During the gas making process, condensation created moisture, which in turn found its way into the mains. The water was collected in special underground traps that had to be pumped out on a daily basis in order to prevent the gas flow being blocked by a backflow of excess fluid. This operation was also carried out at several other locations in the town.

Some smaller local concerns, including the Bengullion Lemonade factory, Campbeltown Laundry and the abattoir offered employment and, while the opportunities may have been limited, it was work nonetheless.

An option taken up by a fair number of local men was agricultural labouring on the numerous farms surrounding the town, another industry in which automation has meant a drastic reduction in the number of manual workers employed.

The unloading of cargo vessels that berthed frequently at the Old Quay was undertaken by a team of dockers supplied by the fuel and shipping agents of C.and D. McEachran, Longrow, the chief stevedore being John *Jock* McMillan.

Around a dozen people were employed in the two cinemas, while hotels, cafes and pubs accounted for another 80 jobs.

A huge contract to upgrade the runways and buildings at RAF Machrihanish was awarded to the well known Wolverhampton-based firm of Tarmac in the late 1950's and many workers signed up to take advantage of the bonanza wages being paid. Some of the men actually moved away from the area at the completion of the contract to continue working for the firm elsewhere.

An even bigger construction job, which commenced in 1963, lasted a long time and was the source of prosperity for all kinds of tradesmen and labourers. Melville, Dundas and Whitson, Civil Engineers, and Mitchell Construction arrived in Campbeltown to build several massive oil storage tanks on Kilkerran hillside and a jetty at Glenramskill capable of berthing ocean-going tankers. In addition, a five-mile long pipeline was laid from Kilkerran to the regenerated RAF Machrihanish to carry aviation fuel to the base for use by NATO aircraft. The site soon became known as *doon the rodd* and the expression has been used on countless occasions in Campbeltown ever since.

The Jaeger Clothing Factory is, thankfully, still in existence and provides vital jobs for a substantial workforce. Opened in 1955 on the site of the former Albyn Distillery by Andrew Douglas Ltd, *The Factory*, as it is known, has been one of the few post-war commercial enterprises to meet with continued success in Campbeltown. Long may it continue in production, because should anything untoward occur at Jaeger, the effects on the town's already fragile economic state would be disastrous.

Another notable employer, which today still shines amid the gloomy industrial scene in Campbeltown, is the prestigious Campbeltown Creamery, makers of delicious cheeses that are on sale nationwide on the shelves of major supermarket chains. It is a pity that the town cannot attract more solid businesses such as this and Jaeger in order to offer some form of employment stability.

THE RETAIL SCENE

Long before the advent of supermarkets in Campbeltown, there were actually 14 dedicated grocery shops in the burgh, while a number of smaller general merchants carried food lines also.

James Gulliver, who had a second grocery shop at Broom Brae, owned the Main Street premises presently occupied by Victoria Wine. The late James Gulliver junior, the famous supermarket magnate, began his working life as an errand boy in the Main Street store. Gulliver's shop became known as The Delicatessen in the late fifties and Mrs. Elizabeth Finn took over at Broom Brae.

The busy and well-known Lipton's Grocers traded from a prime Main Street position in what is now a combined grocery/video rental /off-licence. Lipton's had a travelling shop, a big green Bedford that was driven for years by Dougie McDonald. It was in this shop, that I first saw a portion of cheese being hewn from a huge block by a staff member using a thin garrotte-like wire. The female assistants were always dressed in smart uniforms and funny little hats similar to those worn by nurses. Other memories of Lipton's include the spotless black and white tiled décor and the strong brown paper bags, almost of a soft cardboard quality that were used to package many loose items which nowadays are all checked, weighed and prepacked on factory production lines.

At the foot of Main Street, where today's racing punters place bets in Archie McKellar's turf accountancy, Joe McIlchere and staff ran one of two family shops, the other being at the junction of Longrow and Lochend Street and which now lies empty. Morris McNair in a trusty green Bedford Dormobile van undertook McIlchere deliveries.

Alastair McConnachie had a real old fashioned grocer's shop at the Glebe Street/Big Kiln/Burnside intersection. Cured sides of bacon wrapped in fine muslin hung from the ceiling and certain dry stores were kept in bleached hessian sacks that sat against a wall on the scrubbed wooden floorboards. Gleaming brass weights were used to balance out the required quantities on ancient, but accurate, swing bar scales. Biscuits of all descriptions were stored in shiny square metal tins with hinged glass lids to enable easy identification of the contents.

The brothers Davie and Alastair McEachran had a new shop built in 1958 to replace an old building that had been pulled down at the junction of Longrow and Burnbank. The demolition work created a new street that linked Longrow and Kinloch Road. Until then, the thoroughfare along the side of Mafeking Place as far as Bolgam Street had been no more than an alleyway known as Mafeking Lane. Many fishing boat skippers favoured this shop when ordering stores and the provisions were delivered directly to the vessels at the Old Quay. Extensive deliveries were also made to customers throughout the town.

The shop reopened each day at around 8pm to sell the Glasgow evening newspapers *Evening Times* and the long defunct *Evening Citizen*. Visiting Irish fishermen took advantage of the late opening to stock up with groceries.

On Sundays, Davie drove the familiar light blue Dormobile to Carradale, where a comprehensive range of newspapers and sweets were offered for sale.

Two sizeable grocery stores stood a short distance apart in Longrow, opposite McCallum Street. They were the businesses of Sam Clark and Colin Campbell. Sam Clark also dealt fairly extensively in pet food and accessories.

The Dalintober and Askomil areas were served by J.P.Morton's shop, situated on the corner of George Street and High Street. It is still in existence, trading as Black of Dalintober.

The ubiquitous SCWS had three strategically placed grocery stores in Campbeltown. One was sandwiched between the Lipton and McIlchere shops in Main Street, another midway along Longrow and the third at the top of Broom Brae, adjacent to the Glen Scotia distillery. In addition, several SCWS vans roamed the town and surrounding countryside.

There were two slightly more up-market establishments in business – Eaglesome and A.D.McNair.

The Eaglesome shop was known as an *Italian Warehouse* and I well remember the delightful smell within its confines of freshly ground coffee beans mingled with the pungent aroma of exotic cheeses, herbs and spices. Eaglesome stocked a wide variety of the more expensive grocery lines, fine wines and spirits.

A.D.McNair's shop, the proprietor of which was Mr. Robert Salmon, was run on similar lines, with the exception of alcohol sales.

Campbeltown's traffic congestion today is a nightmare compared to the substantially fewer motor vehicles - especially private cars - that plied the burgh's highways and byways forty years ago. However, it was possible to obtain petrol and oil from no less than six outlets, a far cry from the solitary filling station presently operating in the town - a situation that puzzles me somewhat.

Argyll Street, opposite the White Hart Hotel's public bar, was the setting for Duncan Ramsay's garage, now used as a workshop and offices by the joinery firm of McKinven and Colville. The petrol pumps were actually situated inside the premises and careful negotiation was required when reversing out of the garage to regain the street. Ramsays also dealt in new and used cars, mainly Ford, spare parts and other motoring accoutrements.

The building now occupied by the ATS tyre company in Burnside Street was owned and run as a filling station by the McConnachie family of the Argyll Arms Hotel. A wide range of accessories was on offer here too.

Neil Paterson's Garage in Longrow was another popular fill-up spot. Car sales, repairs and valeting were carried out here and the business still functions today, minus the petrol pumps.

About 150 metres along the street from Paterson is Campbeltown's only petrol supplier, the County Garage Esso Shop, which ceased to function as a garage some considerable time ago. In days gone by it was the fully operational Lorne and County Engineering Company's County Garage, under the direction of Lennox Harrison. Repairs, breakdown service, new Vauxhall car dealing and spare parts sales accounted for much of the County's business.

Long before the days of paramedics, the town's ambulance service was based there. A well-known driver was Donnie Kennedy, a man who did not believe in the unnecessary use of screaming sirens. The odd occasion on which the klaxon was heard signified a call-out of some severity.

Jack McRobert operated the Millknowe Garage, now Glenside Tractors, which was built on the fringe of the Calton estate. As well as petrol and car sales, the Millknowe specialised in heavy vehicle recovery and plant hire.

John Huie's garage was situated in Kinloch Road and, again, sold petrol, accessories and carried out repairs. Huie's supplied a considerable amount of agricultural machinery to the farming community. The building continued to function as a garage under the ownership of Charles McMillan until its closure on his retirement in the summer of 2000.

*

Campbeltown's butcher meat was supplied by a total of six shops, the busiest of which was probably David Kerr, in Main Street. How I disliked standing in a seemingly endless queue in this shop waiting to hand over my mother's order line. The tedium was relieved only marginally by watching the white-coated butchers– who were considerable in number – skilfully honing the fearsome looking boning and slicing knives to razor sharpness by using a dextrous and speedy criss-cross method between blade and steel rod.

Neil McGeachy's shop was in Cross Street and, like David Kerr, he also ran a mobile butcher's shop. Neil catered for the fresh meat needs of the visiting Portavogie, Northern Ireland, fishing fleet.

There were no fewer than four butcher's shops in Longrow South and Longrow. William Renton traded from the premises now occupied by Neil McGeachy's son, Sweeney. Renton's travelling butcher's shop was a familiar sight on the roads, especially in the Carradale area.

Farther along Longrow proper, the firm of Weir is still trading. The late Willie Mitchell, who was, until an advanced age, a keen long distance cyclist, owned this business before his daughter, Agnes, and husband Alastair Stewart took over. They have recently retired and Mr Leonard Gilchrist, who has spent his entire working life there, now runs the shop.

A few metres past Weir is an architect's office. This was formerly McArthur the Butcher, and was looked after by George and Jenny McKay.

The SCWS had a quaintly described *Fleshing Department* in Longrow, a few metres short of its junction with Well Close, the narrow thoroughfare that runs to Glebe Street.

*

The baking trade was well represented, and shoppers could choose to visit any one of six outlets. Each one displayed a tempting array of plain and fancy treats such as cakes, biscuits, buns, rolls, bread, pies and sausage rolls.

The McArthur family, whose bakehouse in Burnside Street has been converted to a ship chandler's store, had two shops – in Union Street and Longrow.

The bakery trading as John Hoyne was actually owned by Mr. John McCallum, the shop and separate display window being in Main Street with the bakehouse to the rear. Access to the ovens was through a close that led on to a right of way through backcourts, exiting in Kirk Street.

Another bakery belonged to Mr.Ronnie McSporran and his shop was in Longrow in the immediate vicinity of the current Golden Ocean Chinese Restaurant. His bakehouse, too, was situated at the back of the premises at the end of a large close.

The SCWS bakehouse in Shore Street is now a car repair business. Goodies from this bakery were retailed in a Main Street shop and from a mobile unit.

Probably the best wedding cakes in Campbeltown were made in the Saddell Street bakery of Joseph Black. This small family business also had a deservedly high reputation for the quality of savouries such as pies and sausage rolls.

Pre-wrapped sliced bread had by this time made a considerable impact on the retail baking business but the Campbeltown bakers continued to produce a limited quantity of plain and crusty loaves. Rolls, of course, were turned out in abundance and it was fairly easy to identify individual bakeries by the texture and taste unique to each one.

Another popular breakfast item was the barm biscuit, a form of morning roll, which was flatter and tasted slightly sweeter. Oven-warmed and spread liberally with golden syrup, a barm was, indeed, a treat to eat.

Tea Rolls, again similar to the morning roll but having muffin-like qualities graced many a Campbeltown tea table.

*

Milk was supplied to the populace by six dairies. Cartons and plastic bottles were an unknown quantity then and many householders in need of a daily supply of fresh milk used special one or two-pint enamel jugs. The jugs, each with a china plate *lid* held in place by a large stone, were left outside each night to be filled with the appropriate amount early next morning. Milk roundsmen, accompanied by young assistants eager for pocket money, transferred the milk from a special container that looked like a billycan with a tight-fitting lid.

The Barbour family, of Hillside Farm, delivered milk in Campbeltown from a horse and cart and I can only just remember seeing the rig in the streets. My memories are much clearer, though, of the five remaining milk suppliers.

Davy Black, a dairyman whose premises were in Kirk Street also used a horse – called Paddy – and cart for transport. Although Davy delivered milk on an early morning round commencing at half past five, he made occasional afternoon forays to collect milk money due to him, and his presence was announced by a shrill blast of the special referee's whistle he always carried.

Another travelling dairyman was David Patrick, who lived at Stewarton and had his business, too, in Kirk Street. David drove a maroon Morris 1000 van, the rear interior of which was almost entirely given over to a big shiny milk tank with brass taps and fittings.

I have vivid memories of the pain inflicted by a long-suffering mother on my nine-year-old bottom in the immediate aftermath of an incident concerning David's milk van, which was parked on the slope outside our Ralston Road house. David was some distance away engaged in conversation with a householder when I, for some inexplicable reason, turned on one of the brass tank taps. The resultant cascade of milk panicked me so much that, in my haste to turn it off, the tap jammed.

By the time David realised what had taken place and managed to stem the milky flow, several gallons had been lost. I can still see in my mind's eye the white stream gurgling its way downhill to the nearest sewer grille.

The loss was estimated to be in the sum of 30 shillings (£1:50p), the buying power of which in those days was substantial, and it represented a considerable slice of my mother's weekly budget. The appropriate reimbursement was made and the sorry scene that ensued indoors completely evaporated my interest in brass milk tank taps! Black's Dairy in Main Street was run by Mrs. Margaret McKellar and is now a toy and souvenir shop. Mrs. McKellar delivered her milk in a beige Ford Popular or Prefect car.

The SCWS, naturally, had a dairy also, which sold bottled pasteurised milk and was delivered by a special van, but the overall preference then was for fresh milk.

Mrs.Polly McShannon, of High Street, lived in a flat above her dairy. Her delivery boys took milk to the Dalaruan, Dalintober and Askomil areas of the town.

It is interesting to note that every shop which dealt in food or other household commodities employed a delivery boy, in some cases two or three. Commonly seen in Campbeltown were the specially made *message bikes*, invariably painted black and equipped with a large square or rectangular wicker basket fashioned to sit inside a framework in front of the handlebars. A plate fitted between the crossbar and pedals was usually signwritten with the owner's business details.

Roll boys with McArthur, Ronnie McSporran and the SCWS, however, were driven round the town and housing estates in delivery vans, such was the extent of early morning custom.

*

Newspapers, periodicals and stationery requisites were available in five newsagent shops.

Provost Archibald Keith ran two, both in Main Street. Number 22 is still in business under George McMillan's ownership and the other, smaller shop later became a menswear store called The Man's Shop. Incorporated in this business was a photographic studio and a limited amount of commercial printing was undertaken.

Almost directly across Main Street from *Top Keith's*, at its junction with Cross Street, is the shop which traded under the name of A.G.Ralston, although it was a gentleman by the name of Smith who owned the shop in my younger days,

The recently closed *Campbeltown Courier* front shop in Longrow back then was only half its present size but was nevertheless a busy retail outlet.

The building that housed the remaining newsagent's shop, owned by Mr A.Greig, was demolished many years ago to make way for the Burnside car park.

There were five gents' barber shops scattered throughout Campbeltown. Attending to the tonsorial needs of the male populace were Peter Finnie in High Street; Bobby McLean in Burnside Street;

Dan Morrison in Longrow; Donald Downie in Hall Street; Bobby Houston in Saddell Street.

Shoe repairs were carried out at four locations. Joe Morrans had a shop in Burnside street, Alastair Graham was based in Shore Street, Sweeney McGeachy in Union Street and Neil Kennedy, per Willie Galbraith, at Cross Street.

Shop frontages in Main Street and Longrow have changed dramatically over the years and, unfortunately, it has to be said that despite valiant efforts by some shopkeepers, there is a look of economic depression in the central shopping area. I am saddened as I write to record the lamentable fact that there is a plethora of empty and boarded up premises in Campbeltown.

It may be pertinent at this point to embark upon an evocative stroll up and down Main Street and along *The Lang Rah*- Longrow's local name - to rediscover the shops and businesses that supplied all manner of products. Naturally, a few may have changed ownership or, indeed, type of stock carried, during the years I refer to in this book but the various retailers mentioned are as I remember them. Details of present day shop occupancy were correct at the time of writing.

MAIN STREET, left-hand side looking towards Castlehill.

At the head of the Old Quay where the Woolworth store stands imposingly, the original building contained a fruit shop, fresh fish shop, a tea-room, Beth McKinven' first fish and chip shop and the Campbeltown and District Savings Bank – predecessor of the TSB bank in Bolgam Street. The various Town Council administrative offices were upstairs.

H.MCILCHERE AND SON. This was the shop occupied by Joe McIlchere as his main grocery. Present occupancy: Archie McKellar's bookmaker shop.

SCOTTISH CO-OPERATIVE WHOLSESALE SOCIETY. The shops in this stretch of Main Street, numbers 11 – 17, belonged to the SCWS, and included a menswear department, bakery, dairy and large grocery store, which was the town's first self service. Present occupancy: clothes shop, fancy goods store and crafts shop.

DAVID KERR. Mrs Flora Kerr's butcher shop traded here for many years before the business closed down and became a pharmacy. Present occupancy: Moss Chemists.

JOHN HOYNE. The numbers 21 - 29 were partly embraced by residential property and the bakery business of John Hoyne. Present occupancy: grocery and fast food outlet owned by McGeachy Foods.
THOMAS LIPTON. Lipton's grocery, which later became a branch of the Galbraith chain. Present occupancy: Archie McKellar's grocery, off-sales and video shop.
THE TOBACCO HOUSE. The Tobacco House was a truly singular tobacconist's shop and belonged to the wholesale tobacco and confectionery distribution concern of Richard Daniels and Company. This firm was controlled by Mr. James Daniels senior, an astute businessman, and employed a considerable number of warehouse and office staff at its Old Quay Head premises. The building was demolished in the mid-nineties.
A vast selection of cigarettes, cigars and tobacco were stocked in the Main Street shop. Snuff was sold in tiny quantities and I can remember the delicate little set of counter scales used for this purpose.
The Tobacco House also dealt in high-quality smoking accessories such as lighters, pipes, cigarette cases and holders. Two huge shiny chromium plated cigarette vending machines were bolted to the wall at the entrance to the shop. One contained plain cigarettes such as Capstan Navy Cut, Players and Senior Service and the insertion of a silver half-crown piece (twelve and a half pence) produced a packet of ten. Tipped cigarettes including Bristol, Embassy, Kensitas and Sterling could be had for a florin (ten pence). Present occupancy: empty.
THE SCOTCH WOOL AND HOSIERY STORES. As the name suggests, an extensive range of wool, threads, material and other sewing requisites were available in *The Wool Shop*, which was subsequently owned by Galls. Present occupancy: Dan Morrison & Co, Jewellers, run by the late Mr Morrison's daughter, Una.
A.KEITH. Photographic portraits and the printing of tickets, small catalogues and leaflets comprised part of the business of this stationery shop, which was one of two owned by former Provost Archibald Keith. Present occupancy: part of the Victoria Wine shop.
JAMES GULLIVER. It was here, in the humble surroundings of his father's grocer's shop, that James Gulliver junior began his career in the food business. He was destined to become chairman of the huge Argyll Foods conglomerate.

Mr. and Mrs. David McPherson later ran the shop as The Delicatessen. Present occupancy: the main premises of Victoria Wine.

MAYFAIR CAFÉ. At the junction of Main Street and Kirk Street stood the Mayfair Café, a busy establishment owned by Oswald Grumoli. The Mayfair was one of three traditional Italian-style cafes in Campbeltown which specialised in home-made ice cream, confections, snacks, teas and coffees.

The deliciously milky coffee was made by using a noisy steamer that scalded a milk/coffee mixture and formed a frothy top on each cupful.

The Mayfair had an upstairs department that was a traditional meeting place for some of the sportier young people and, indeed, one of the most successful sides in the local amateur football league, Mayfair Thistle, was formed in the *Top Mayfair*. There was also a badminton competition trophy known as the Mayfair Shield.

The café's interior was very much Art Deco, incorporating dark wood panelling, chrome, glass, and a stone floor of colourful design. Present occupancy: was until recently a ladies fashion shop but has now ceased trading and lies empty. The first floor was converted into a Chinese restaurant several years ago but has been closed down for some time.

BOOTS THE CHEMIST. Next door to the Mayfair Café was a pharmacy that belonged to the famous Boots chain. The store was split into two parts by a common close leading to upstairs flats. As I write, I can almost smell the pleasant fragrance of soaps, scents and oils and taste the special Boots boiled sweets – an occasional treat – that were covered with a very fine type of sugar and sold in ornately-painted round tins. The decision to close the Boots Campbeltown branch was met with considerable dismay by townspeople. Present occupancy: A.P. Taylor, Menswear.

GENERAL POST OFFICE. The last building in Main Street, at its junction with Argyll Street, blighted the landscape and was a bone of contention for 30 years or so. This boarded-up and neglected edifice, which served admirably as Campbeltown's General Post Office until the late sixties, has, thankfully, been recently partly renovated. A new state-of-the-art P.O. building was erected at nearby Castlehill but the *new* premises now also lie forlorn and empty, thanks to the Post Office's removal to the CO-OP supermarket at Rieclachan.

Coming back down into Main Street from the abandoned Post Office, the attractive honey coloured stone building which formerly housed the Royal Bank of Scotland is now occupied by the well-known law firm of Stewart, Balfour and Sutherland.

THE CLUB. At the top of Main Street proper, the imposing and architecturally attractive red sandstone headquarters of The Club stands testimony to an era of considerable prosperity in Campbeltown. Known widely - and inaccurately - as *The Gentlemen's Club,* its membership at one time consisted mainly of affluent industrialists, businessmen, and fellows of the various professions. However, its doors are open nowadays to a clientele drawn from a more general walk of life.

ARGYLL ARMS HOTEL. The Argyll has in recent years embraced the former bus office and waiting room that was sited next door to The Club.

A.G.RALSTON. Past the Argyll Arms and the Town Hall, at the junction of Main Street and Cross Street, this former newsagent's shop has traded under a variety of guises since the retirement of its owner. Present occupancy: empty.

MARY WILSON. This shop has been kept in the Wilson family, though used for two very different purposes. It was formerly a ladies hairdressing salon run by Mary Wilson. Present occupancy: Alec Wilson's butcher shop.

MACKELLAR'S DAIRY. Mrs Margaret MacKellar had her dairy here before Mrs Rene Coffield became proprietrix and ran it as a ladies boutique. Present occupancy: D.M.Brown, toys and souvenirs.

THE TV AND RADIO SHOP. Arthur Strain recognised the potential offered by the electronic revolution that was sweeping the world and commenced business in this shop under the banner of *The T.V. and Radio Shop.* He stocked a comprehensive range of electrical goods, including record players and discs. It was here that I bought by first-ever 45rpm celluloid single, red-hot from the Parlaphone factory. Present occupancy: fast food outlet specialising in baked potatoes.

WALLACE. Mrs Wallace offered confectionery and ornamental fancy goods for sale in this interesting shop, which later became the Kintyre Lounge Bar. Present occupancy: part of Drummonds Lounge Bar and Discotheque.

KINLOCH BAR. On the corner of Main Street and Longrow South, before this business became the combined pub/disco it is today, Tom

Douglas ran the very successful Kinloch Bar. It was a well-patronised traditional public house with a horseshoe bar and could be accessed from both Main Street and Longrow South. I remember an amusing true story which involved a couple of pals who were having a clandestine drink in the Kinloch when one of them noticed the other's wife, obviously harbouring portentous suspicions as to her husband's whereabouts, entering by the Longrow South door. Fortunately, the men were partly hidden by a partition and one, leading the way to the Main Street entrance, whispered urgently to the other: "Quick, McK...This way to safety!"

JOHN HODGE. On the opposite corner site, extensive selections of jewellery and fancy goods were stocked here in the premises of John Hodge. Mr Hodge was also an optician and supplied townspeople with spectacles and other ophthalmic needs. This shop could also be entered from Main Street and Longrow South. Present occupancy: The Courier Centre.

EASIPHIT. This shop belonged to the shoe chain company of Easiphit, the spelling of which always intrigued me. It was possible to obtain certain items of footwear here – albeit sometimes with lesser-known trade titles – considerably cheaper than names such as Clark or Lotus, which the shop also stocked. When I reached the stage of having to pay for new football boots myself, I was inclined to patronise Easiphit. The inevitable short life of the much-used boots, of course, painfully highlighted the folly of indulging in false economy. Present occupancy: The Chocolate Box, a delightful little sweet shop run by Mrs. Marion Russell, which I am glad to say has reverted to stocking traditional confections from the era referred to in this book.

E.PATERSON. Mrs Elizabeth Paterson dealt in a variety of babies and children's wear, other light clothing, wool, buttons and thread in this shop which was eventually taken over by George McMillan next door.

GEORGE MCMILLAN. Formerly A.Keith's, George has been in business here since the late former Provost Archibald Keith's retirement many years ago.

A.P.MACGRORY. One of Campbeltown's continually successful retailing outlets, the former Provost of the same name owned A.P.MacGrory. MacGrory's shop sold television sets, radios, electrical goods, records and sporting goods and in recent years has branched into footwear, clothing and fancy goods, with stocks on two floors. Present occupancy: the business is still known as A.P.MacGrory, under the ownership of Mr and Mrs Hugh Hall.

K.MARTIN. Mrs Efric Wotherspoon, now in her eighties, has retired from her bookshop, which trades under the name of K. Martin. She has had the shop, which also deals in stationery and greeting cards, for decades. Mrs Wotherspoon, though no longer actively involved, is the only surviving shop owner in Main Street carrying on business in the same premises since 1960.

STORE. This shop, which was used for many years by the firm of Richard Daniels and Co. as an annexe to the main warehouse at Old Quay Head, is now known as Main Video and stocks a comprehensive selection of videotapes and other television accessories. It has to be said that its present appearance compares favourably with the drab frontage that was prevalent for a long time.

R.S.MCCOLL. Another well-established Scottish retail chain, R.S.McColl, which deals in confections and newspapers, had a shop here. Following the firm's withdrawal from Campbeltown, a gentleman called Frederick G.Herd ran the premises as a confectionery before it became a fashion boutique. Present occupancy: showroom for paintings and drawings.

G.HUNTER. The one time base of Gordon Hunter, a former *Scottish Daily Express* photographer, who moved to Campbeltown and set up a photographic business in the early 1960's. Gordon covered most local weddings and had a studio in Burnside Street where he undertook portrait photography. He also took all the press pictures for the *Campbeltown Courier*. Present occupancy: empty.

LONGROW SOUTH, left-hand side, looking west. The corner premises formed part of the Kinloch Bar and is now part of Drummonds.

JAMES THOMSON. Jimmy Thomson dealt in fresh and smoked fish, fruit and vegetables both here and in a second shop in Burnside Street. He also sold fish from a big green painted mobile shop, which was driven by Drew Stewart.

J. AND M.MCIVOR. Mr and Mrs Jimmy McIvor ran this fruit and vegetable business as a family concern and traded for many years, latterly in premises across the street.

BANK OF SCOTLAND. It was around this time that the Bank of Scotland moved its offices from Castlehill to Longrow South. The last occupant of this shop was the firm of A.D.McNair. The bank also eventually took over the shops that were originally occupied by Jimmy Thomson and J. and M. McIvor, the last tenant being confectioner Finlay Borthwick.

A.H.FLEMING. This was Archie Fleming's main chemist's shop, which carried a range of toiletries, pharmaceutical products and so on. He was also a dispensing chemist used by the local doctors. Present occupancy: Moss Chemists.

VACANT. The shop next door to the chemist was the only one out of the entire expanse of Main Street and Longrow that I remember as being empty, but on at least two occasions during the run-up to Christmas, toy shop owner Duncan Brown used the window to display a magical array of novelties that kept my nose pressed to the glass! Present occupancy: part of Moss Chemists.

DOCTOR'S SURGERY. Doctor Sandy Cameron had his practice here, before being succeeded by Dr Bill MacDonald. Present occupancy: empty.

DICK AND MCKELVIE. The corner premises at Longrow South's junction with Union Street were the offices of the legal firm presided over by senior partner Alastair McKelvie, and latterly by Robert Graham, who was also Burgh Prosecutor. Present occupancy: insurance office.

HYDRO-ELECTRIC BOARD. Strictly speaking, the offices of the NoSHEB were actually in Reform Square, across Union Street from Dick and McKelvie, though the building's frontage is on *no-man's land* between Longrow South and the beginning of Longrow. Present occupancy: split between a ship chandler's store and recently opened gents' hairdressing salon.

THE MAN'S SHOP. The able businessman *Big Alex* McMillan stocked good quality gents and boys clothing here. I always remember the shop being packed out when back to school day approached towards the end of the summer holidays, as mothers kitted out male offspring with the necessary uniform. Present occupancy: soft furnishings shop.

GALBRAITH AND COCHRANE. The long established painting and decorating firm was run by the brothers Alan and Tom Cochrane from this, the end shop in Reform Square. It is still in business today as a paint and wallpaper retail store but there are no longer any journeymen painters employed.

LONGROW: ELLIS. The first shop on Longrow proper at its junction with Burnside Street was a traditional little sweet shop owned by the Ellis sisters in which a mouth-watering selection of chocolates and candies were sold. Present occupancy: small novelty and sweet shop known as The Corner Shop.

ELIZABETH MACVICAR. Owned and managed by the lady of that name, this shop dealt in ladies and girls clothing. Present occupancy: ladies hairdressing salon.

J.MCNAIR. An ironmongery, hardware and fancy goods store commonly known as *Johnny Nerr's*, the shop had a faithful patronage among the farming and fishing communities. Its owner, Michael Brodie, was hugely popular with his customers. The shop is known today as The Hardware Store and is owned by the late Michael's son, Neil, who deals mainly in household and fancy goods.

CLYDESDALE BANK. The situation of the Campbeltown branch of the Clydesdale Bank has remained unchanged for many years.

KENNEDY. Frank Kennedy was the proprietor of this shoe shop, which has has undergone several changes of use over the years. Present occupancy: now called Penny Lane, the shop sells a selection of light household goods, gifts and souvenirs at affordable prices.

D.MORRISON. There can be few Campbeltown men or boys from this era who did not visit the barber's shop owned by the late Dan Morrison. Charlie McFadyen, who still has a small salon in Kirk Street, ably assisted Dan in what was easily the busiest men's hairdressing business in town. My boyhood haircuts in this shop always culminated in a liberal – often requested – application of Brylcreem or a generous drop of an aromatic lotion called Bay Rum. The slicked-down Adolf Hitler look easily distinguished a youngster newly emerged from Dan's shop. Present occupancy: Credit Union office.

D.MCNAIR. Visits to this little shop-cum-office in wintertime were always welcome. It was here that payments due to the coal supplier D.McNair were made. There was a permanent warm glow inside during the colder months thanks to a big coal fire that was kept well stoked. Present occupancy: empty.

A.D.MCNAIR. This was the site of the already mentioned grocery store owned by Mr. Robert Salmon. Present occupancy: empty.

WEIR: One of the few remaining business still trading in Longrow since the 1950's, this butchers occupies two shops separated by a close, one of which is used as a store.

LONGROW CHURCH ENTRANCE. This space was enlarged in the late 1950's, a casualty being Hugh Clark's tearoom, which was demolished.

MCARTHUR, BUTCHER. On the demolition of the tearoom, this became the gable end property immediately west of the church gates. Present occupancy: architect's office.

CATHIE THOMSON. Another source of great delight to youngsters, this sweet shop sold a variety of popular confections, including numerous *penny trays*. Present occupancy: part of the same architect's office.

N.L.MCMILLAN. Originally a fully operational gents tailoring business with substantial rear workshop and fitting-out rooms, *NL's* eventually switched to the retailing of ladies and children's clothing. Neil McMillan's son, *Big Alex* of The Man's Shop, later tastefully converted the spacious backshop into a private dwelling house. Present occupancy: toy shop.

SCWS. The next three frontages, known as the *Co-operative Buildings*, were occupied by the SCWS as a grocery store, shoe shop and small dairy. Present occupancy: petshop/haberdashery with Crocks Emporium household goods store next door.

ARGYLL HEALTH BOARD OFFICES. The Health Board's administrative staff occupied at least two frontages. Present occupancy: also part of Crocks Emporium.

SCWS FLESHING. The Scottish Co-operative Wholesale Society's butcher shop. Present occupancy: Kintyre Youth Advisory office.

W.G.PROSSER. Willie Prosser was the manager of this firm of slaters and plasterers, which also dealt in light building materials, fireplaces and monumental stones. It was situated at the junction of Longrow and The Well Close, the wide alleyway leading to Springbank Distillery. Present occupancy: private dwelling.

SAM CLARK. This grocery shop was the first retail unit past The Well Close, being preceded by the Springbank Gospel Hall and the building firm of R.Weir. Present occupancy: annexed to Duncan McMillan, House Furnishers.

OFFICE ACCOMMODATION. Present occupancy: empty.

C.MCMILLAN. Yet another small sweet shop was in business here and was well patronised by Millknowe Primary Schoolchildren. Present occupancy: small office belonging to Springbank Distillery.

NEIL PATERSON. Neil Paterson began by repairing and dealing in agricultural machinery but later expanded into the private car sales and repair market. This was his first new car showroom and embraced McMillan's sweet shop on its closure. Present occupancy: empty.

COLIN CAMPBELL. A fairly large double-windowed grocery shop, which employed several assistants, traded here. Present occupancy: vetinerary practice.

THE WALLPAPER SHOP. First established many years ago by the late Mr Alec Martin, this home decorating supplier is now run by his daughter, Mrs Agnes McAllister.

J.MCLEAN. This busy little general merchant's shop was known throughout the town as *Renee Clane's*. It was run for many years by Mrs Renee Davidson (nee McLean, hence the shop's byname) and her brother, Neil. Long opening hours attracted considerable evening custom. Renee and family took over the Dellwood Hotel some time ago and the shop passed to other owners. Present occupancy: empty.

GPT. A firm called General Piped Television arrived in Campbeltown in the late 1950's to create a common television reception service from a main mast set up on the hillside at Crosshill. For a reasonable weekly fee, local subscribers were linked to the mast. The shop was taken over by Rediffusion and then by Radio Rentals. Present occupancy: empty.

A.H.FLEMING. The second, smaller shop that belonged to chemist Archie Fleming was situated here. It supplied mainly ophthalmic requirements and was equipped with eye-testing facilities. Present occupancy: empty.

ARMSTRONG. At the gable end of the building immediately west of the vacant lot that was to become Neil Paterson's garage and showroom, this was a combined confectionery/fish and chip shop, which also drew considerable custom from the schoolchildren of Millknowe and Dalintober Primaries. Present occupancy: private dwelling house.

JOHN PATERSON. At the top of Longrow, at its junction with The Roading where the Co-operative supermarket now stands, there was a huge furniture shop and showroom owned by John Paterson. The

business also included funeral undertaking and upholstery work.
John Paterson's shop and a private 1930's bungalow type house were
demolished to make way for the Co-op store's car park.

It is now time to cross the road and continue our stroll eastwards, or
back down Longrow.

H.MCILCHERE AND SON. This shop, which was originally a
grocery store and then became linked to an adjoining bakery, closed
down some time ago and is presently in a neglected state.

MITCHELL'S BAR. Past the housing blocks of Park Square, at
Longrow's junction with McCallum Street, the late Howard Ward
ran this busy public house. Present occupancy: Kilbrannan Bar and
Oliver's Lounge Bar.

GARBUTT PAINTERS. The small painting and decoration firm of
Garbutt occupied this shop before becoming part of Duncan
McMillan's present business.

DUNCAN MCMILLAN. As well as dealing extensively in house
furnishings, Duncan McMillan was also an upholsterer and
undertaker.

MISS FINNIE. This ladies hairdressing salon also later became part
of the expanding business of Duncan McMillan.

SCOTTISH GAS BOARD. The Gas Board's showroom doubled as
an office where gas bills could be paid. Gas fires and cookers were
displayed here. Present occupancy: empty.

RONNIE MCSPORRAN. Tasty items from Ronnie's bakery at the
rear of the shop appeared daily in the display window here. Ronnie
left the town eventually and the business was turned into a fish and
chip shop. Present occupancy: part of the Golden Ocean Chinese
Restaurant.

JOHN SHIELDS. *Jock* was a well-liked figure, especially by
children, who described himself as a radio and cycle agent. He dealt
in new and second-hand bicycles, radios and televisions and was also
a boat hirer. He was in great demand when the current primary
school fad demanded ownership of a catapult, or *sling,* as we knew
it. For the entirely affordable sum of one old penny, Jock used pliers
to fashion a bicycle spoke into an excellent framework to which was
attached a series of elastic bands joined together. Ammunition
supplies were easily procured by the utilisation of cardboard bus
tickets that were tightly folded into pellets. The creation of this lethal
weapon took mere seconds but it could inflict stinging injuries on

enemies that lasted much longer! Present occupancy: extension of Golden Ocean.

DO-IT-YOURSELF SHOP. This small DIY store was opened by Malcolm Martin in conjunction with his joinery business and traded for several years before being altered to become the Kintyre Farmers electrical goods department. Present occupancy: bicycle shop, although it is presently up for sale.

JOHN HUIE Hardware, ironmongery and fancy goods were sold on two floors here. The store was part of the Huie's Garage business on Kinloch Road and was later taken over by Kintyre Farmers. Present occupancy: empty.

QUINN & CO. The brothers Dominic and Leo Quinn owned this marvellous double shop that kept all types of leisure, work and sports equipment/clothing, including footwear. There was always an interesting smell on the premises – an amalgamation of leather, rubber and new cloth. The Quinns were true gentlemen, generous to a fault, and were known to kit out, free of charge, entire boys' football teams with strips. Various tenants have come and gone since the Quinns retired, when the shop was split into two and used for other purposes. The brothers were greatly missed by customers and the business community alike when ceased trading: Present occupancy: recently renovated as an optician's consulting rooms and shop.

CAMPBELTOWN SAWMILL. This business was situated in a yard accessed by the wide close next to Quinns. Run by the Mauchline family it was a joinery firm that also turned out timber commodities such as fence posts, garden sheds and other items for the agricultural community. Present occupancy: store.

R.MCARTHUR. Baking produce was delivered to this shop by van from the McArthur bakery in Burnside Street. The McArthur family had two shops and employed about a dozen people. Present occupancy: Neil Kennedy's shoe shop.

M.MCDOUGALL. Miss Maimie McDougall had a small haberdashery store here. Present occupancy: the shop was included in recent major extension work carried out by the Robertson Electrical and Household goods store.

D.M.BROWN. Small this shop may have been, but it represented an absolute wonderland for wee boys like myself and, on reflection, a place of dread for my mother. To me, this was *THE* toyshop in

Campbeltown, a veritable grotto stocked to the roof with a massive selection of playthings that were guaranteed to intoxicate any child. As a youngster, I could never understand why my mother mostly chose a pedestrian route that left Duncan Brown's shop at a safe distance! Now and again, though, the promise of "a toy" guaranteed impeccable behaviour for days before the eagerly anticipated excursion took place. Birthdays, trips to the dentist or special occasions were usually marked by an exciting visit to this place of dreams. Present occupancy: also part of the Robertson store.

MARY MCCALLUM. This little sweet shop occupied by old Mary McCallum was the last business premises in Campbeltown to be lit by gas and has also been swallowed up by Robertson's. Mary used to freewheel to the shop each morning on an ancient bicycle from her house at Hazelburn and walk the machine back home at night!

R.A.WALLACE. The big shop owned by the Wallace family was run latterly by the brothers, Jack and Robert. It stocked furniture, electrical and fancy goods. Funeral undertaking and upholstery work also formed part of the business. Present occupancy: the shop was taken over a few years ago by the aforementioned Robertson Electrical firm, which has branches throughout central Scotland.

ROLLAND AND POMPHREY. Mr Bob Dobbie, assisted by Mr William Mustarde, ran a chartered accountancy from this office. Present occupancy: ladies hairdressing salon.

J.FERGUSON. Mr Jack Ferguson was in business here as a jeweller, watchmaker and stockist of fancy goods. Present occupancy: empty.

ROBERT ARMOUR AND SONS. Owned by Mr Hugh Thomson, this plumbing and ironmongery firm employed nearly 30 tradesmen, apprentices and shop assistants. The shop also sold hardware and fancy goods. Present occupancy: the shop is divided between a busy photography studio and a former Chinese takeaway that has lain empty and neglected for a long time.

WEST COAST MOTORS. It was from this parcels office and waiting room that the familiar red and cream West Coast buses departed for destinations such as Carradale, Southend and Lochgilphead. Present occupancy: the bus office was taken over by The Campbeltown Courier during renovation work and incorporated in the new front shop.

THE CAMPBELTOWN COURIER This is where the local newspaper was printed and published whilst under family ownership.

The author pictured at work on board the Caledonian MacBrayne car ferry 'Lochranza'.

An aerial view of Campbeltown. There are still numerous whisky bonded warehouses in evidence.

The 'Kirkin' o' the Council, 1957. From left to right: Provost Anthony MacGrory; Sheriff R.Millar; J.Morton, Town Clerk; Bailie John Anderson; Burgh Treasurer Wiliam Stevenson; Bailie Malcolm McCallum; Dean of Guild Daniel McKinven; Councillor Archibald Keith; Councillors John Scott, Flora Kerr and Sandy Ross.

A huge fleet of herring ring net boats pictured at The Old Quay, Campbeltown. Note the steamer passenger turnstile huts on the pier.

'Cleaning time' for the ring net fleet. The boats were positioned in such a way that they became high and dry at low tide. The Rex Cinema in the background was still attracting big audiences but was closed in the late 1970's and later demolished.

Campbeltown lifeboat (reserve vessel) at her New Quay moorings. Berthed at the Old Quay in the background is the TS 'Duchess of Hamilton', which was a regular visitor for many years.

Lifeboat coxswain Archie Malcolm is pictured here beside the town's regular lifeboat, 'City of Glasgow 2', which was commissioned in 1953.

Council dignitaries and Salvation Army officials at the annual Service of the Sea weekend.

Provost Archibald Keith welcomes HRH Queen Elizabeth 2 and the Duke of Edinburgh during the Royal visit of 1958. The Royal Yacht 'Britannia' was anchored in Campbeltown Loch.

A few of the hardy men employed at the Argyll Colliery. This photograph was taken underground and shows (back, l to r): Duncan McInnes and Bill Livingstone. Front, l to r: Bertie Cook; William McKinlay; Wattie Campbell; Robert Martin and Angus Gilchrist.

The smiling faces of the Campbeltown Salvation Army Choir in the days when the local corps had a full strength band as well.

Pictured in Hall Street outside A & P McConnachie's bus office in Hall Street is one of two double-deckers that ran in the town in the early 1960's.

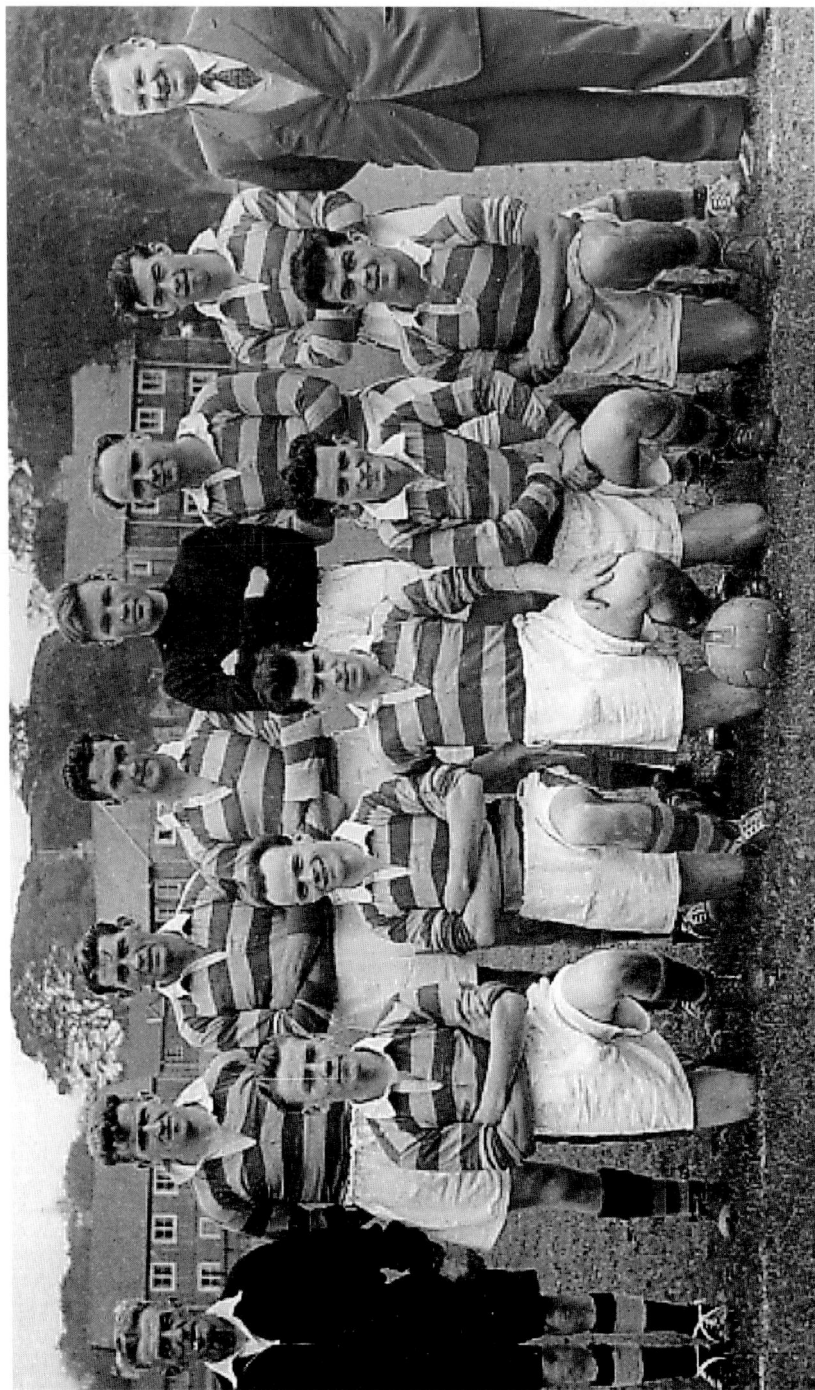

This select side turned out for Campbeltown in a representative football match in 1960. Back row, left to right: Referee Archie 'Purba' Mustarde; Donnie Kelly; Hughie Newlands; Neil Watson; Archie Simpson; Sandy McGeachy; Neil Martin; Councillor Archie McCallum. Front, left to right: Tommy McGeachy; Charlie McFadyen; Jim Martin; Malcolm McPhee and Donald Mustarde.

The popular Dalintober Beach, Campbeltown, is now sadly barren and abandoned and calls have been made for renewal work to be carried out.

The ring netter 'Nobles Again', aboard which I spent many happy boyhood days at the herring fishing with my Uncle Tommy.

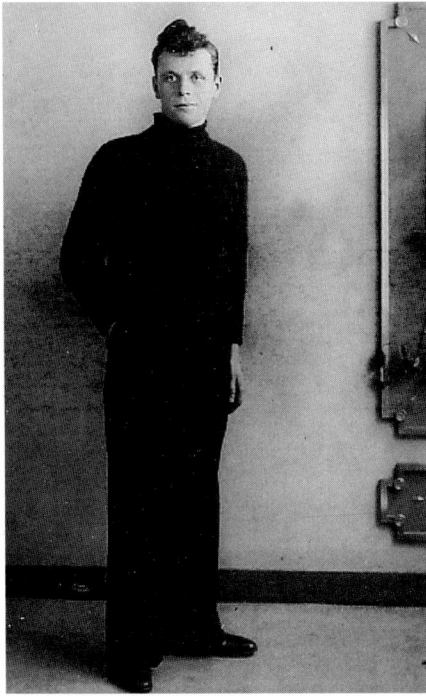

Uncle Tommy in his younger days dressed in the Campbeltown fishermen's 'Saturday morning' outfit

The men of the 'Stella Maris', who showed great kindness to me on my early fishing trips. Back row (l to r): Jackie Paterson; Campbell McBrayne; Joe Brown and Denis Meenan. Front (l to r): Donald Munro and Skipper Jim Meenan.

George McMillan was one of several boatmen involved in ferrying tourists to Davaar Island and the famous cave painting of the Crucifixion.

The Davaar Island rock face painting of the Crucifixion, which caused a sensation when it was discovered in the late 1800's. A local artist, Archibald MacKinnon, following a visionary dream, painted it.

The universally known Manfred Mann beat group pictured with staff in Campbeltown's Argyll Arms Hotel in August 1964. Their blockbuster hit 'Do-wah-diddy diddy' went to No 1 in the UK charts on the same day the band was playing the Victoria Hall.

Perhaps they were not quite as famous as Manfred Mann, but this Campbeltown group, The Sceptres, were popular throughout Argyll in the 'swinging sixties'. Left to right: Danny Black; Sammy Duncan; Kenny Johnston; Davie Brodie, Flo McLellan and Andy Donaldson. Neil Brodie is at the drums.

The busy front shop was staffed by five assistants and carried a big stock of newspapers, magazines and all kinds of stationery requisites. The printing room was situated at the rear of the building and could be accessed from the Burnbank area. Present occupancy: empty.

ALEXANDER MCEACHRAN. The brothers Davie and Alastair McEachran ran their grocery business from this Longrow-Burnbank junction shop. Present occupancy: the shop was converted into the Dhorlinn Restaurant and Takeaway but is now closed down.

SCWS. The Co-operative furniture and fancy goods store occupied almost the entire ground floor of this building known as Mafeking Place. Doctors Colin McKenzie, Ian MacPhail and Archie Wallace used a small part of the floor space as consulting rooms. Present occupancy: jointly used as a health food store and a sports shop.

EAGLESOME. The Italian style delicatessen still trades under the same name but is principally a liquor off-sales outlet.

LONGROW SOUTH: LANG HAIRDRESSER. This was probably the largest ladies hairdressing salon in town, employing several girls. Present occupancy: building society office.

DONALD GILCHRIST. Popular fishmonger Donnie Gilchrist moved to this shop when the Old Quay Head building was demolished to make way for the new Woolworth building. Present occupancy: now known as The Fish Shop, Mr and Mrs Archie McMillan, of Carradale own the business, though Donnie is still to be seen in the shop frequently.

LIVINGSTONE. Mr David Livingstone ran this well patronised ironmongery and hardware store for many years. Present occupancy: fruit and vegetable shop known as Fresh Connections.

WILLIAM RENTON. Renton's butcher shop was one of the six trading in Campbeltown at the time. It is still in business under the ownership of the McGeachy family.

P.H.TAYLOR. A general selection of clothing and millinery was available here before the shop was sold. Successive retailers trading under different guises have owned the shop the over the years. Present occupancy: empty.

LOCARNO CAFÉ. The Locarno was one of the three Italian cafés and was highly popular. It was owned by Mr and Mrs Jack Togneri, the parents of local artist Ronald. Mrs Togneri's toasted sandwiches were in great demand as were the gargantuan ice-drinks and sundaes made with the Locarno's own ice cream. The Togneris also stocked a vast selection of sweets and boxed chocolates that were displayed on wall mounted glass cabinets. Present occupancy: it is still a café but offers only limited confectionery and snacks and is a mere shadow of its former self.

SCOTT'S BOOT AND SHOE SHOP. This was the shop that Mr and Mrs Jimmy McIvor moved into following the Bank of Scotland's take-over of their premises on the other side of the street. Present occupancy: still trades as a greengrocery under different ownership.

CENTRAL TEAROOM. Queues formed outside this homely little eating place each day at lunchtime, such was its reputation. The Central was owned by Mrs Netta McLachlan and, on the odd occasion in my case when the partaking of a school meal was necessary, I sideswiped the bland Grammar School dining hall fare for the much more acceptable and tasty soup and main course which could be had here for the juvenile concession price of 1s 6d (all of twelve and a half pence). The seductive aromas that radiated from the premises when cooking was in progress is another fond memory. Present occupancy: empty.

STANLEY NOAL. Noal's was another dedicated tobacconist's shop owned originally by the gentleman of that name. The shop sold cigarettes, tobacco, snuff and a range of pipes, lighters and so on. Present occupancy: computer accessories shop.

JOHN HODGE. The Longrow South side of the corner shop at its Main Street junction formed the other part of John Hodge's business. Present occupancy: The Courier Centre.

There were, of course, many other shops outwith the *main drag*.

In fact, well in excess of 100 retail outlets offering a diversification of commodities traded in the Royal Burgh.

A large tenement structure with shops on its ground floor stood on the site of the Burnside Square car park. Mr A. Greig, newsagent and stationer, owned the corner shop of this building, which faced the Feathers Inn – then the public bar of the Argyll Arms Hotel. Mr Greig had a private library at the rear of the shop and he lent out books at a cost of 3d (just over 1p) per copy. Roy Watson occupied the Union Street frontage in The Campbeltown Fruit Market along with James McGeachy who had a large ironmongery store next door. McGeachy's shop strangely enough, also served as Campbeltown's

first travel agency. Other commercial units in the building were
James Grant, electrician and Neil Kennedy's footwear repair
workshop, which was affiliated to the Cross Street shop.

On the Longrow South side of the block, across Harvey's Lane, the
SCWS ran a store that dealt in household goods and was known
curiously as the City Warehouse.

Opposite The Campbeltown Fruit Market were the premises of
R.McArthur, bakers, Nan MacKay, ladies fashions and a ladies
hairdressing salon.

The railed-off open area to the rear of the TSB Bank was the site of
an old three-storey building that was in an advanced state of decay
and had dark, foreboding closes. There were two shops between this
unsightly cavern and the Eaglesome delicatessen.

Shoemaker Sweeney McGeachy, a man whose talented hands also
produced many fine models of sailing ships and fishing vessels -
some of which could be seen on the premises - occupied one.

William Robertson, alias Dirty Bill, was the owner of the other
shop, a dingy little emporium which was, to say the least, interesting.
Dirty Bill's unchanging garb was cloth cap, glasses, and overcoat.
He usually had a cigarette stub in his mouth and dealt in sweets,
tobacco and limited grocery lines. Magazines of a more adult nature
could be purchased there as well.

Dirty Bill's was a favourite haunt of schoolboys from Campbeltown
Grammar when it came to exchanging empty lemonade bottles for
single Woodbine cigarettes. Slightly unhygienic and cluttered the
shop may have been, but he knew precisely where everything was.
It came as a shock to many that, when the shop was cleared out on
Dirty Bill's death, a considerable amount of money was discovered
stashed among the sweet jars and cardboard boxes.

Both shops have now been combined to create the Campbeltown
Pottery.

Mrs Tina Wardrop had a quaint little shop in Pensioners' Row,
opposite the offices of the Job Centre at New Quay Head. The shop
was actually a room in her house and I used to call for sweets if I
happened to be in the area. Sometimes Mrs Wardrop would be *ben
the hoose* preparing a meal or baking and the smell of home cooking
wafting through the passageway greatly increased my desire for
confectionery. Mrs Wardrop was another splendid storyteller who
could hold the undivided attention of my young mind. There was

also a fine little grocery and general merchandise store at St Andrew's Square, Shore Street, which was owned by Mr Bob Mitchell, before being taken over by George McMillan, who also ran a mobile shop.

Handy little general merchants served the housing schemes. Ted Fleming had a small wooden chalet-type shop at Albyn Avenue in the days of the prefabs; Fred Waggett was in business at Glentorran Place and Jack and Jessie MacRobert built the Ralston Road shop, which is still trading under different ownership after more than 40 years.

The Lochend, Saddell Street and Dalintober areas were well catered for by retailers. The McIlchere family had a shop at the junction of Longrow and Lochend and the redoubtable Jack McKinven's fully stocked general store was in Saddell Street, across the road from Morgan McAllister's Glue Pot pub. Joe Black's delightful bakery business was housed a few metres along Saddell Street, directly opposite the famed McKinlay's fish and chip shop, next door to which was an electrical goods store ran by a man called Findlater. This shop later became Bobby Houston's hairdressing salon.

Towards the junction of High Street at Broom Brae there is now a fenced off open space that is used as a yard and warehouse access by the Glen Scotia Distillery. Here stood the shops of Mrs Elizabeth Finn and Miss Jessie Cook, along with the adjacent SCWS grocery and butcher branches on the High Street corner beside the distillery. Further along High Street were the businesses of Bob Johnston, general merchant; Polly McShannon; J.P.Morton; Miss Hyndman in the sub-Post Office; and barber Peter Finnie. Turning into Princes Street, Colin Martin had a clothes shop beside the Queen Street junction. With the exception of the chip shop, Morton's and the sub P.O., all of the business premises mentioned above have either been demolished or are lying empty.

As I got older, frequent calls were made to a quiet little shop tucked away in Kirk Street. This was where Tommy Murray, a friend of my father and experienced saddler, worked in leather. Tommy's trade was dying quickly, thanks to automation on farms, and I was glad to have been able to see a true craftsman at work before he shut up shop for good.

Hall Street, or *The Front*, as Campbeltonians prefer to call the area, was home to the Grumoli family's revered Royal Café. The Royal, next door to the Christian Institute was a favourite haunt of the fishermen but also had a loyal clientele drawn from other townspeople. The Royal, run by the ageing Leo Grumoli and his son, Robert, had a deserved reputation for cleanliness and efficient service and their homemade ice cream was in popular demand throughout the year.

The Grumolis held court over much of the property along the commercial part of Hall Street in the building known as Royal Avenue Mansions. Mrs Dora Kennedy (nee Grumoli) ran the Gift Shop next door to the café and Lydia Grumoli's shoe shop was next in line, followed by Dora's acclaimed coffee shop and restaurant known as The Copper Kettle. The premises later became an Indian Tandoori restaurant, the trading arrangements of which have become somewhat irregular.

Between The Copper Kettle and The Picture House cinema's confections kiosk were the British European Airways booking office, a bus office and Donald Downie's barber shop.

The age of Rock 'n Roll had arrived in Campbeltown and teenage lads keen to get in vogue by dressing in the recognised garb of drainpipe trousers, crepe-soled shoes, leather jackets and fluorescent socks needed to look no further than the premises of clothier Alec Bryson, whose store was at the Bolgam Street-Burnbank junction. Alec was the saviour of many youths when he introduced a club system of paying for the goods, some of which were of poorer quality and a bit garish; but it was what the youngsters wanted. His made to measure Italian style suits, though, were fashioned in a superior material and sold well. The trendy Campbeltown youth of the early 1960's wore winkle-picker shoes with pointed toes, an Elvis Presley style haircut held in place by Brylcreem or Silvikrin and an Alec Bryson Italian suit.

Alec, whose prized possession was a 2.8 bright red Jaguar with wire wheels, died whilst still fairly young and his shop was converted into a public house, yet another business that has been closed down for some time.

THEY ARE NO MORE

Several prominent buildings that were very much part of the
Campbeltown landscape around 1960 either have been demolished
or dramatically converted for other use.

At the junction of Kinloch Road and Burnbank, on the site of the
attractive council flats known as Kinloch Place, stood a big tenement
with the grand name of Kinloch House. An imposing building,
indeed, it was a local landmark when viewed from seaward coming
up Campbeltown Loch. The ground floor of Kinloch House was
latterly the office and workshop of an electrician's business. The
flats built on the corner to replace Kinloch House were much sought
after due mainly to the block's central, but fairly quiet, location and
the pleasant views of the harbour and loch that can be enjoyed from
the houses.

Directly across Burnbank from Kinloch Place, on the other corner
site, are several privately owned apartments. This building was
previously known as the Albert Hall, scene of many rousing gospel
meetings in days gone by, though Messrs Charles Flaws and John
Shaw, netmakers and repairers, last used it.

The ground floor area of the building during its ecclesiastical period
was the venue for Campbeltown's weekly livestock auction market.
A wide close-type opening led to holding pens at the rear of the
premises and the animals were brought inside to the auction ring
through a series of railed-off passages. School holidays usually
meant a Monday visit to the mart by friends and myself and
memories remain of the rather questionable combined bouquet of
cattle dung, sawdust and pipe tobacco smoke that pervaded the
atmosphere.

A few metres past the Albert Hall, beside the Victoria Hall, was the
Joseph Gundry Networks, which had a massive interior stretching
back to the rear entrance in Bolgam Street. The factory's demise
began in the late 1960's and was eventually closed down completely
in the seventies, when the building underwent sweeping conversion
to become the workshop, offices and showroom of the Campbeltown
Motor Company. The motor firm has since moved to modern

purpose built premises at Snipefield and the former factory is now
empty and up for sale.

The Christian Institute, which stands sentinel at the head of the Old
Quay, is known as the *YM*. Said to be the town's tallest building, it
was erected many years ago during Campbeltown's most prosperous
period as the headquarters of the local YMCA (Young Men's
Christian Association). Following the rundown of the YMCA, the
YM was seconded to Campbeltown Grammar School as an annexe
for physical education classes. Around this time, thanks to the
sterling efforts of Councillor Archie *Baldy* McCallum, a Sunday
night youth club was established. This proved to be extremely
popular among teenagers and allied organisations including a
formidable amateur soccer team, drama club and badminton squads
were formed. The interior housed a dance floor, stage and balcony as
well as side rooms, small shop, football dressing room and a
committee room. Following considerable conversion, the *YM*
nowadays fills a very different role and is used as the area offices of
Argyll and Bute Council, West of Scotland Water and the Social
Work Department.

At the other end of Hall Street, midway between the Campbeltown
Library and the Labour Exchange, the wonderful Rex Cinema
commanded an excellent waterfront location overlooking the inner
harbour. The white-painted Art Deco building was demolished in the
late 1970's - yet another victim of the UK public's preference for a
diet of mass television.

The 1200 - seater picture house, which was owned by the major
leisure firm of Greens, thrilled thousands of cinemagoers during its
40-year life, including hordes of children at the Saturday matinees. It
was the venue, also, for variety shows and concerts and at one time
had a self-contained café in operation.

 The late Tommy Duff, whose keen wit was noted in Campbeltown -
especially if he had partaken of a dram - managed the Rex for many
years. Two other well-known employees were projectionists Tommy
Galbraith and Ian McAulay, who sometimes relayed popular music
to summer holidaymakers on the seafront via loudspeakers set up
outside the top floor projection room.

An invitation to the pictures when boy met girl was an easy chat-up
line and many a romance was consolidated high in the balcony's

better seats that we knew as the golden divans on a Friday or Saturday night, with little interest being shown in the feature film! The Rex could be seen from sea through the gap between Davaar Island and Glenramskill with such clarity that Campbeltown fishermen used the building, lined up with other topographical features, as a transit mark when shooting white fish seine nets in order to prevent the gear coming in contact with a particularly bad section of rocky seabed. This fishing operation was known as *the picture-uss haaull* and saved many a net from being torn before the days of electronic navigation aids.

I was part of a crowd of townspeople which formed when the heavy demolition gear moved in to reduce the cinema to rubble in a matter of hours; a sad day indeed.

The site of the Rex is now occupied by a recently built nursing home, an attractive building in itself, but the former cinema car park has been left as an unsightly weed-bound fenced off area littered with building materials. I very much doubt if such an eyesore would be tolerated on a seafront anywhere else, especially if there was a ferry terminal used almost exclusively by holidaymakers only yards away.

Although it is still standing, the Templars Hall at Millknowe is in a dreadful state. Known more commonly as *The Bowery*, this pleasing stone building was built in 1871 and run by the International Order of Good Templars.

In its heyday, dances and concerts were held in the spacious hall and market traders used the floor space for one-day sales of clothing and household goods. However, the gradual deterioration of *The Bowery* in recent years has gone unchecked and it now requires extensive renovation.

Not far from *The Bowery*, across The Roading, a prominent edifice known as Millknowe Primary School blended with the western skyline. Generations of youngsters including myself were educated there. On the completion of the modern secondary school at Limecraigs, junior classes were united in the former Grammar School buildings by the formation of the new Castlehill Primary and Millknowe was, consequently, closed. The building remained in a boarded-up state for a while before the decision was made to demolish it and the cleared site became part of the Scottish Gas LG storage plant.

Two other conspicuous tenement buildings, both of which housed many families, were situated in the Dalintober area. On High Street, at the top of Broom Brae, is a vacant site on which once stood a greystone block named Gayfield Place. And further west on High Street, at the rear of Dalintober Primary School, was another large tenement known as Cowdenknowes. Arthur's Seat was the unusual description given to a row of small houses between the Cowdenknowes and Dalintober School.

I can just remember the Lynn Hotel, which was situated in Shore Street before it was demolished to make way for the building of a new public house called The Clachan. The bar has had several name changes since and is presently known as Whisky Mac's. I seem to recall that the Lynn Hotel was a temperance establishment, where alcohol was unavailable.

Perhaps the most controversial demolition job in recent years was the razing of the beautiful Lochend United Free Church to make way for the Tesco supermarket car park in Lochend Street. The supermarket building was constructed on the site of an adjoining whisky warehouse that was also demolished.

It is an unfortunate fact that dwindling church attendances have become prevalent throughout society on a nationwide scale. Campbeltown is no exception and the Lochend was apparently quite seriously affected, a matter which led to the eventual cessation of services in the church. It lay empty for some time before the decision was made to bulldoze the tasteful building, resulting in the loss of yet another important local landmark.

RELIGION AND EDUCATION

In 1960's Campbeltown, it was possible to worship God and take part in affiliated activities in no less than 12 religious institutions, including five Presbyterian Churches of Scotland.

The various ministers were familiar figures in the town and spent a lot of time visiting parishioners. The clergymen I remember were Rev. John R.H.Cormack, Castlehill; Rev. Ivan F.Tibbs, Longrow; Rev. G. Stuart Cameron, Highland Parish; Rev. Ewan McLean/James Hood, Lorne Street; Rev. James Young, Lochend; Rev. John Ferguson, Free Church; Father James Webb, St. Kiaran's R.C and Rev.A. A.Mills, St. Kiaran's Episcopal.

However, the universal decline in congregation numbers and interest shown in the Church's work has ultimately affected the Royal Burgh, resulting in a greatly reduced level of spiritual proceedings. Of the five major churches, only two remain – Lorne and Lowland and the Highland Parish.

The first victim of the decrease in attendances was Castlehill Church, built overlooking Main Street on the site of an ancient castle. The congregation amalgamated with Longrow Church to form the new Lowland Church and the building was later bought by a construction firm for conversion into luxury flats.

Next to close was the Lochend Church, as has been mentioned, followed by the Lorne Street Church, which is now the town's Heritage Centre. An impressive display of local artefacts and photographs is on show here as an excellent supplement to the Campbeltown Museum, but the grounds surrounding the building have been allowed to become untidy and overgrown, resulting in a somewhat uninviting appearance.

On Lorne Street's closure, the congregation united also with the original Longrow Church and the new Lorne and Lowland came into being.

The other religious houses that have ceased to function are the Albert Gospel Hall and the International Order of Good Templars hall at Millknowe.

Still very much on the go, however, are Campbeltown's Free Church of Scotland at Dalintober, St. Kiaran's R.C.Church, the Episcopal Church, Salvation Army and Springbank Gospel Hall.

The churches and other religious organisations, of course, offered members more than just the traditional Sunday service. Every church had a hall that was utilised by a Sunday school, Bible Class, Women's Guild, Men's League and badminton club. Carpet bowling was another popular weeknight activity, especially in wintertime. The Salvation Army Citadel in Burnside Street was the venue of an over-sixties club called the Harmony Hour that was run for years by the late William Anderson. My friends and I attended occasional film shows, albeit local amateur productions, in the Citadel, an added attraction being the traditional handout of an iced bun and small bottle of lemonade. Similar goodies were available, too, on Kinloch Green when visiting evangelists held open-air services during the summer holidays. The meetings were held in the Albert Hall if it was raining.

The education set-up was slightly different than it is today, since the proposed new box-like concrete and glass Campbeltown Grammar School building wasn't even on the drawing board. Part of the original Grammar is now known as Castlehill Primary School, which was created to accommodate pupils from Millknowe Primary. It was seen as a sensible move since much of the Millknowe intake was from a catchment area close to Castlehill. Primary one and two classes, formerly taught in the Grammar School annexe commonly referred to as The Wee Grammar, were included in the new format. St. Kiaran's Primary was moved to the vacated annexe, which suited its needs better than the rather cramped accommodation previously occupied in Kirk Street.

Dalintober Primary, with Millknowe, formed the school known as Kinloch Primary although the buildings were sited about three-quarters of a mile apart and the football teams vied with each other constantly for supremacy; the annual sports meeting was another day of intense competition. Today, however, Dalintober is a primary school in its own right.

The various youth organisations can, I suppose, be loosely connected to the education of youngsters, and the different bodies were extremely well represented in Campbeltown.

The Wolf Cubs, under the guidance of Ian Brown, shared the John Street hall with the Boy Scouts, who at that time were run by Dan Galbraith and Arthur Muir.

The Lifeboys and the Boys' Brigade were affiliated to the Lorne Street Church and were supervised respectively by the Misses Margaret McArthur and Flora Henderson and Mr.John Hall. The B.B. also had a recreation hut in Ralston Road.

Captain James Skedd looked after the local Army Cadet Unit, whose parades were held in a new Ralston Road hall while their maritime opposites, the Sea Cadets, had David Farmer and Robert Salmon as leaders at T.S.Campbeltown, Kilkerran Road.

The Air Training Corps, led latterly by John Gillespie were based in timber-built headquarters at the rear of John Paterson's furniture store at Rieclachan before new premises were built beside Castlepark. The older lads in the ATC were often given the opportunity of going aloft in training aircraft and the unit had a talented pipe band.

The Guides and Brownies had substantial membership and many girls joined the local detachment of the Junior Red Cross.

The annual November Armistice Day Parade to the war memorial on The Esplanade was an important occasion then, when all the youth organisations joined senior Army, Navy and RAF personnel and the Ceannloch Pipe Band in a march to commemorate the men of Campbeltown who fell in action during the two World Wars.

TRANSPORTATION

I count myself lucky to have been around when most of the vehicles now known as *classics* were already negotiating the roads of Campbeltown and the Kintyre Peninsula.

I would hold that the modern design features of lorries, buses and, perhaps to a lesser extent, cars have created an almost monotonous similarity in appearance and it can be difficult at times, for me at any rate, to readily identify some of the shapeless machines seen on the highways today.

As a youngster in the fifties and sixties though, I could reel off the different vehicles' trade names instantly on sight, such were the distinctive looks and engine sounds applicable to each one. I can also remember many of the three letter registration marks.

Lorries manufactured by Swedish, Dutch and German firms were unknown in the area and goods vehicles displayed ornately fashioned maker's plates bearing British names representing Albion, AEC, Foden, Bedford, ERF, Leyland, Seddon, Commer or Dennis. The famous and totally reliable Gardner engine, built at Patricroft, Manchester, powered many of the goods vehicles.

Similarly, the sighting of a Japanese or Italian light commercial vehicle in Campbeltown then would have been a rarity. Austin, Commer, BMC, Bedford, Morris or Ford were the main suppliers in those days. And, of course, private cars came from UK plants of companies such as Austin, Rootes, Ford, Humber, Wolseley, Vauxhall, Morris, or Rover.

Road transport from the central belt to Campbeltown in the earlier part of the century posed little opposition to the established and efficient service provided by the small coasting vessels that sailed from Glasgow. In the 1920's and early 1930's the road hauliers used steam-driven outfits called Sentinels that were built at Polmadie, Glasgow. My grandfather, Bob Gillies, drove one that towed roadmaking materials and a corn threshing machine to various Kintyre farms at harvest time.

The Sentinels used two hundredweight of coal during the two day trek between Glasgow and Campbeltown, and had great difficulty negotiating several one in six gradients en route, notably Rest and Be

Thankful, Cairndow, Clachan/Whitehouse and between Muasdale and Glenbarr, However, road improvements and the introduction of the HGV- a *monster* at seven tons – signalled the beginning of healthy competition between the shipping companies and road hauliers.

Government legislation, however, decreed that any journey outwith a 20-mile radius from recognised bases such as Campbeltown had to be undertaken by 'A' Licensed nationalised transport. The famous state controlled British Road Services was formed in 1948 and the local branch of BRS Argyll came into being by the take-over of Kintyre Road Services, whose garage was at The Roading. Throughout the next two decades, the Campbeltown depot of the BRS grew in strength to become an important local employer and more than 30 lorries were based at the spacious new garage on Kinloch Road. The BRS fleet consisted mainly of red - painted Albion, Leyland, Seddon and AEC models ranging in size from four to 14 wheelers. On denationalisation, the transport unit became known as SRS West, but later vanished into the sunset.

Although there was a 20-mile limit in force, several local firms nevertheless operated as general carriers and certain exemptions were granted for the long distance carriage of commodities such as fish and livestock. There were more than 100 drivers in Campbeltown by 1960.

Duncan Ramsay, as well as running his Argyll Street garage, had two trunking Gardner-powered Albion lorries that were used prior to the implementation of the new rules and several smaller Ford Traders with V7 petrol engines replaced them. The green painted lorries, with eye-catching rear sloping radiator grilles, were a familiar site on the country roads around the town as they went about their business carrying milk churns to the local creamery. The Ford Traders were kept in garages - long since demolished to make way for private apartments - opposite Stewarts Green beside MacGrory's Nursery. The Campbeltown and Machrihanish Light Railway Company had previously used the buildings as locomotive sheds. Ramsays also ran a larger three-axle Fordson that was used to transport whisky barrels from puffers at the Old Quay to various warehouses in Campbeltown.

The uplifting of full milk churns, which were left on special platforms at farm road ends, also provided work for smaller lorries belonging to Gavin Henderson, John Huie and McKerral of Southend. Gavin later sold his long-nosed Bedford to the expanding McFadyen's concern. Farmers residing within a few miles of the town usually took the milk to the creamery themselves in carts pulled by either the ubiquitous grey coloured Ferguson T 20 tractors or Clydesdale horses.

Milk from the dairy herd at Drumore Farm, on the outskirts of Campbeltown, was taken for processing by two bonnie little Bedfords that had been bought by farmer Andrew Smith as surplus stock from the War Department. One of the trucks was completely refurbished in a livery of chocolate brown with gleaming chrome wheeltrims and hubcaps. It was driven by 17-years-old George Harvey, who has gone the full circle and now collects milk for the creamery in one of Bibby Distribution's tankers after having spent a lifetime behind the wheel of all types of lorries.

James McPhee, grandfather of the present proprietor of the Burnbank Garage and Tyre Depot, also carried milk churns in a Bedford (SB 9725). He later obtained two BMC K7 models that were used for, among other things, livestock transportation before being replaced by two Leyland Comets (DSB 12 and DSB 13). McPhees also ran a BMC minibus (CSB 511), believed to be the first of the modern type in Campbeltown.

John McLean (*Jocky Clane*) drove an old red painted Bedford with such caution that it appeared never to ascend from second gear! Jocky, who also had an Albion, delivered coal throughout the town and country, one of his runs being to the Mull of Kintyre Lighthouse. How he negotiated the perilously steep and twisting road to the lighthouse in the elderly vehicle was a wonder to many.

Commer marketed a two-stroke flatbed that proved to be a popular three-tonner, probably because it was capable of the then unheard of top speed of 70mph, albeit in an extremely noisy manner. Harvey Giffen, a wholesale fish merchant, had two green Commers and another, resplendent in two-tone maroon, belonged to the Campbeltown Sawmill and was usually driven by Duncan Mauchline.

The building firm of Neil McArthur, whose yard was beside the Unigate Creamery, used two tipper lorries for transporting limestone from a quarry at Ballymeanach to a crushing plant at Fort Argyll. Despite fairly extensive enquiries, I have been unable to identify the make of the fawn-coloured lorries, which were of a rather odd shape at the front, though a possibility is that they were also World War 2 surplus and could even have been of a foreign origin.

John McAllister, then based at Benmore, was a self-employed contractor and a great believer in Bedford lorries. He remained loyal to the company until his retirement, his last one being a TK. John's preferred colour was green and he was also heavily involved in the transportation of whisky barrels and coal from the Old Quay.

The old Argyll County Council lorries used by the road maintenance squads were easily perceived by their grey livery and the occasional presence of a portable workmen's hut on the back. Generally Albions, the council wagons based in Campbeltown carried men and materials to locations on the Kintyre peninsula's roads network.

Kintyre Farmers Limited, the newly formed co-operative, had a green BMC fitted with dropsides that was used to deliver animal feeding and collect eggs destined for its egg packing station at Glebe Street. KF's first driver was Teddy McCallum, who went on to become one of Campbeltown's most experienced HGV drivers, finishing his career with McFadyen's Transport, who, incidentally, bought the original KF lorry as part of its progressive expansion programme. The KF later acquired a larger Bedford GK wagon. Another distinctive regular on the Kintyre highways was the County Garage's grey/blue paraffin tanker, a vehicle that covered many miles delivering the popular domestic fuel to outlying districts.

An orange-coloured Bedford TK flatbed that was driven by Charlie Morrison was seen daily in the streets of Campbeltown. Operated by the bottling firm of Joseph Dunn and Co. from the former Bengullion Lemonade Company's premises at Castleacres, the lorry delivered soft drinks and canned beer to shops, pubs, hotels and cafes.

McFadyens Transport and Contractors, whose business today is impressive, has grown through the years from humble beginnings. Before Archibald McFadyen and Sons obtained its first 'B' Carrier Licence – circa 1955 - the firm used Clydesdale horses and long flat carts. McFadyens road haulage enterprise began with a tipper lorry and expanded steadily to include livestock floats, articulated lorries, construction plant vehicles, animal feed bulkers and timber carriers. Archie McFadyen's brother, Neil, a local coalman, also drove a horse and large cart. In the gathering darkness of winter afternoons during his round, *Neilly Fadjen* as he was known, sometimes borrowed a sharp kitchen knife from my mother to trim the candles which were encased in glass frames and used as coach lights on his rig.

The only goods vehicle operated by West Coast Motors by the mid 1950's was a Royal Mail van, which ran daily from Campbeltown to Glasgow and back. However, when the mileage limit rules on road haulage were relaxed somewhat, the Craig family built up a mixed fleet of commercial vehicles to compete with the BRS, including three Albion Reiver tippers that ran cement to the NATO construction site at Kilkerran. The goods lorries were mainly Bedford, although the heavier stuff came from the Albion stable. Success followed and West Coast Motors bought over the concerns of Ramsay and McPhee before eventually selling out to BRS.

Many people at this time still relied heavily on public transport and two bus companies, West Coast Motors and A. & P. McConnachie operated comprehensive local and rural timetables. It was not uncommon for some peak time services to be augmented by a second bus to cope with passenger numbers.

The continual growth of West Coast Motors over the years has meant the creation of depots in Ardrishaig and Oban and the company's buses can be seen over a wide expanse of rural Scotland and the Glasgow area, being part of the Citylink network. In my younger days, however, West Coast Motors provided a local service, including buses to Tarbert and Lochgilphead, from its garage at Benmhor and office/waiting room in Longrow, Campbeltown.

The company ran with frequency to all the Kintyre villages, with the exception of Machrihanish, and had the education department contract to transport secondary school pupils to Campbeltown and Tarbert from various country locations. Another important part of the service was the carriage of small (some not so small) parcels and daily newspaper deliveries to farms and houses along the route. Rolled up newspapers were fired like missiles through an open window by the drivers with such deadly accuracy that they hardly needed to slow down.

Carradale at the time was a *dry* village with no pub, which could be inconvenient for those who were not averse to a dram or two. As a result, West Coast bus drivers were – particularly on the 4pm and 9pm Saturday runs - recruited by some villagers on a regular basis to obtain and discreetly deliver the amber nectar to Carradale.

The buses that ran to Carradale then were red and cream 29-seater Bedford OB Duples with a curved body and pronounced long-nosed bonnet under which ran a high-pitched engine. I was a regular passenger on the Carradale bus, thanks to frequent family visits to my granny's house in the village, and either Willie Ramsay or Archie Darroch drove the vehicles; one had the registration number SB 7779. Two other drivers seen often on the rural runs were Matt Paterson and Duncan McQuilkan, who drove a Leyland Tiger half-cab and was sometimes accompanied by the firm's only permanent male conductor, Norman Keith (*Wee Norman*).

An incident involving *Wee Norman* on the Carradale bus has been spoken of many times in the village over the years. The driver of the day, Willie Ramsay, had stopped the packed Bedford Duple outside his home at Tormhor, which stood on a slope. The handbrake could not have been fully engaged because, when Willie went in to his house to collect an envelope for posting, the bus began to move downhill. Alarmed passengers implored conductor Norman to halt its progress, only to be met with the oft-quoted reply: "Och, ah canna. I only push the bell!"

Fortunately, one of the passengers saved the day before any damage was done.

West Coast Motors had a policy of employing students during the summer months, the young lads and girls acting as conductors and general *dogsbodies* on the country runs.

The company ran a daily service to Lochgilphead that connected with the Clyde-Tarbert steamer. Calum Kerr drove the long-nosed Leyland Comet used on this route for years before progressing to a newer Bedford.

Private excursions have always been an important part of the West Coast Motors business and all kinds of bookings were taken, including football specials. Rangers and Celtic fans actually shared the same coach often, the only stipulation being that all club colours were removed from sight on the outskirts of Glasgow!

Another regular private reservation came from the men of the Campbeltown fishing fleet if the vessels had been moored for the weekend at Crinan or Tarbert; those runs became known as Fishermen's Specials.

One of the most popular drivers on tours and special journeys was John (*Jock*) McKay, and his name was often requested when bookings were made. On such trips Jock drove a Leyland Royal Tiger bus, which with its slightly curved roof and offset access door, was almost oval in appearance.

The introduction of the Bedford Vega and Bella Vista coaches into the West Coast Motors fold in the mid 1960's was the first of the semi-modern designs to be seen on the roads of Kintyre, and I have to admit to a liking for their looks, which were not excessively box-like.

A. & P. McConnachie, owners of the Argyll Arms Hotel, ran a fleet of buses, tipper lorries and taxis from sizeable garage premises at the rear of the hotel and across the road in Burnside Street.

The company provided an extensive town bus service as well as operating on the Machrihanish and Tarbert routes. During the summer months, McConnachie's buses stood at the head of the Old Quay to await the arrival of the turbine steamers, whose passengers often took advantage of short tours to Machrihanish or Southend.

A certain amount of excitement was generated in 1961 when the first of two AEC double-decker buses, hitherto unknown in Campbeltown, arrived to join the organisation, which at the time was being managed by Duncan McConnachie.

McConnachie's buses were either painted in a livery of silver grey or blue and cream. Other models owned by the firm included Royal Bedford Duples, Leyland Cheetahs, Leyland Royal Tigers, two single-deck AEC's with open rear entrances (BCP 534 and BCP 535) and Leyland Aviation.

Unlike West Coast Motors, this company employed full-time conductresses and some of the young ladies who were on the buses at the time were Jeanette Durnan, Rosie Duncan, Flora Muir, Mary Gillespie and Mary Arkell. Drivers included Reid Thomson, Andy McKinlay, Eddie McMurchy, Lamont McCallum, Mailer Thomson and Laspie McKinnon. The name of another driver, Archie Neill, was synonymous with the daily Tarbert run, on which he plied for many years – latterly in a Bedford Vega coach (ASB 50). Archie and another driver, Ned McSporran, were the last drivers in Campbeltown to wear shiny knee-length leather gaiters, which had been part of the early commercial motorist's uniform.

Another important contract held by the company was the conveyance of Argyll Colliery miners from the town to the

Machrihanish pit. Day shift, back shift and night shift workers were taken to and from work in this way.

McConnachie's buses carried primary schoolchildren, from the Meadows housing estate to Millknowe School – a fair distance – for the princely sum of 2d, which in decimal currency represents about eight tenths of one new penny!

Scottish licensing laws during this period were a bit confusing, to say the least, and alcohol could only be sold to *bone fide travellers* in hotel bars during certain hours on a Sunday. Consequently, thirsty Campbeltonians – predominantly male and in fair numbers it may be said - took advantage of McConnachie's and West Coast tours to various locations throughout Kintyre that had the convenient attraction of an inn. The buses, with destinations chalked on hinged boards, left from *The Triangle*, an area of open ground beside Kinloch Green in the vicinity of the swimming pool.

A. & P. McConnachie also had a fleet of taxis and two Rolls Royce hearses of considerable vintage. Invariably painted black, the taxis were either Austin saloons or of the petrol FX3 London cab type. I recall the registrations of two – a big Austin SB 8000 and an FX3 TLM 750. Arthur Hastie and Alec Stuart were regular cab and hearse drivers.

Alec was nearing retiring age when he picked up his most famous fare. He was told to collect a Mr Taylor and friend from a private aircraft that had landed at Machrihanish Airport. The couple asked to be taken far along the Gobagrennan Road to remote High Park Farm, which was for sale. Not until he had dropped the couple back at the aircraft did Alec realise that he had been chauffeur to none other than Paul McCartney and Jane Asher. The news caused a sensation in Scotland, but Alec remained quite calm; after all, he had only ever vaguely heard of the Beatles!

Another common sight each evening in the Royal Burgh was the appearance at half past eight of the David MacBrayne Glasgow-Campbeltown service bus. The green and red coach, which displayed a claymore-wielding kilted warrior and the famous slogan: *MacBrayne for the Highlands* along its panelling, left Parliamentary Road, Glasgow, at 3pm each day and passengers faced an eventful five and a half-hour journey. The return trip meant a 7am departure from outside the Post Office in Main Street, arriving in Glasgow at almost 1pm. A long wheel based bus built, I think, by Alexander of

Falkirk, replaced the Maudsley model that covered the route for a long time, before the service was taken over by Western SMT vehicles that were painted brilliant white with black trim.

The Royal Hotel, owned then by Archie Malcolm, ran a bus and two black FX3 taxis. The green-painted Bedford Duple 29-seater was permanently chartered by British European Airways for the transfer of passengers and baggage to Machrihanish Airport to connect with the daily Viscount aircraft flight from Glasgow.

As the 1960's progressed, private taxi operators challenged the Argyll Arms and Royal Hotel monopoly. A gentleman of Polish extraction who was known, naturally, as *Jan the Pole* owned the first non-black taxi in Campbeltown. He started off with a two-tone blue Austin Cambridge, hence the name of Blue Taxis, telephone number 2153. Jan was a reliable and popular taximan to whom time and distance was no object and, not surprisingly, his business flourished as locals became more taxi orientated.

Machrihanish man John Marlin, who sadly died while still young, ran two Ford Consuls and Lamont McCallum plied for hire with a big Vauxhall Cresta and Ford Consul (GSB 806). He later acquired a Ford Zephyr 6 and a Humber Hawk (JSB 920), a truly superb car of solid construction which I was privileged to drive as a youthful part-time taxi driver in the years that followed. It is interesting to note that all the aforementioned models had leather bench-type front seats and gear change levers mounted on the steering column. The light green Humber had the added refinements of a highly polished wooden walnut fascia, radio and overdrive control - a device that saved petrol while cruising at speeds of up to 100mph!

More and more large saloon cars with Hackney Licences appeared on the streets of the town throughout the 60's and by the end of the decade there were nearly 20 taxis on the go.

The various emergency service vehicles, the majority of which are now universally painted white with fluorescent red or orange trim, each had a different livery. My earliest memories of the Campbeltown police motor pool are of a Wolseley 444 saloon, Austin Westminster saloon and a Bedford Dormobile Black Maria (GSB 271), all painted black. Later additions were a green Ford Cortina Mark 1(KSB 118), used as an unmarked surveillance car and a dark blue landrover. Constables also rode several black Raleigh pedal cycles and a BSA 250cc motor cycle. Two-way radio sets were still a thing of the future, and a number of police communication boxes fitted with flashing blue lamps at various locations throughout the town kept officers in touch. Also part of the beat constable's regular checks was the observation of a large glass-covered fitting that was affixed high on the Campbeltown Sheriff Court building at Castlehill. If the light inside glowed in a bright red colour, the duty bar officer required the immediate attention of beat Bobbies, usually to furnish details of an incident that required urgent investigation. The fire service headquarters were in a disused distillery building on the site of the present Tesco supermarket before the new Fire Station was built nearby at Lady Mary Row. The two tenders were a Bedford and a fairly new Dennis, which was equipped with an extension ladder connected to a huge wooden spoked wheelbase for ease of manoeuvrability at the scene of a blaze.

Before the blue-painted St Andrews Ambulance Association mercy vehicle – the forerunner of today's models - took up its duties, two smaller coffee-coloured Humber ambulances emblazoned with big red crosses served Campbeltown from the County Garage base. Perhaps my favourite vehicle of the era was a massive grey steamroller – a Fowler– that was to be seen often at various roadworks within the burgh. This wonderful machine, so big in every way, was driven quite expertly by perhaps the smallest of the Council employees, *Wee Ned* Graham, who must have stood all of five feet.

The roller was usually accompanied by a tar boiler when local streets were being resurfaced, a process that included depositing a thin layer of liquid tar to bind grey crushed granite chips that were spread thickly on top. *Wee Ned* in his colossal machine made certain that the chips were, indeed, pressed firmly into place.

Ned's steamroller towed the tar boiler, which resembled George Stephenson's original Rocket locomotive complete with smokestack, at a snail's pace to different locations in Campbeltown.

LEISURE AND
ENTERTAINMENT

The Royal Burgh of Campbeltown was historically the most heavily
industrialised of the Argyll towns, while tourism and ancillary
service industries mainly brought about the development of places
such as Oban, Dunoon, and Tobermory.

Although perhaps not as commercialised as the more established
resorts, the town was, nevertheless, a fairly popular holiday
destination in the fifties and sixties, drawing summer vacationers
from Glasgow, the Central Belt and expatriates from all over the UK.
A great number of holidaymakers arrived on the Caledonian Steam
Packet Company's swift turbine steamers *Duchess of Hamilton* and
Duchess of Montrose, having embarked at the railheads of Gourock
or Fairlie Piers. Others sailed on the David MacBrayne mail steamer,
Columba, which plied between the Clyde and East Loch Tarbert to
connect with West Coast Motors or McConnachie's buses for the
pleasant trip along the Kintyre Peninsula. Some even came by air, on
the big British European Airways Viscount aeroplane that flew daily
from Glasgow to Machrihanish Airport.

However, the appeal of comparatively inexpensive package holidays
to sun-drenched Mediterranean and Canary Islands locations has
meant a reduction in the local and Scottish holiday trade in general.
But I can't help thinking that if Campbeltown was still being run by
a Town Council, especially now that an substantial ferry terminal
and linkspan has been established, greater numbers of holidaymakers
would be attracted to the area.

I don't intend to fall into the trap and say that summers when I was a
boy were invariably long and hot; they were not. But they were
certainly enjoyable and the release from school for a glorious six-
week holiday holds many happy memories, not least because –
thanks largely to the efforts of an effectual Town Council
Entertainment Committee and a specially appointed Entertainment
Officer – locals and visitors of all ages had plenty to do. Leisure and
entertainment activities were enjoyed in an almost carnival
atmosphere created by the long string of coloured lights that curved

around the lochside from Dalintober to the paddling pool at the Quarry Green.

There were two busy putting greens on Kilkerran Green, while the municipal tennis courts at Kinloch Green directly opposite the Lochend Church attracted a more energetic clientele.

The two local bowling clubs welcomed visitors on to their greens and, as now, golfers could choose between the championship links at Machrihanish, Southend's Dunaverty course, or the friendly nine-hole Carradale club.

The local bus companies ran special excursions and services to the outstanding beaches at Machrihanish, Westport, Southend, Peninver and Carradale. In good weather the man-made Dalintober Beach at the head of Campbeltown Loch was positively alive with sunbathers and swimmers.

Boat hiring from the inner harbour slipway or learning how to handle a kayak in one of John Shield's flotilla at Dalintober appealed to many. And countless holidaymakers were ferried to Davaar Island in well-maintained launches to marvel at the cave painting of the Crucifixion, an awesome experience indeed.

Mackerel fishing from either of the two quays or from small boats was another popular summer pastime and organised competitions were held. Some of the more junior fishermen were content to hook the *cuddies,* or *gleshans* (small saithe), which shoaled in vast numbers among the *skeegs*- a Campbeltown description for the massive wooden supports of the Old Quay. Fly fishing permits, which allowed anglers to visit various well-stocked lochs around the town, sold well in selected local shops.

Lots of holidaymakers spent unforgettable nights as skippers' guests at the herring ring net fishing or on day trips to the prawn trawling.

A Civic Week organised by the Town Council which involved dances, concerts, children's beach competitions and sports events culminated in a Saturday Gala Day, when an impressive and colourful procession of lorry tableaux, usually headed by the current Miss Campbeltown and her attendants, wound its way through the town's crowded streets. Spectators showered the vehicles with bronze and silver coins and the coffers of various charities benefited accordingly.

In the evening, a huge crowd watched a programme of inner harbour water sports and other aquatic activities from the quaysides and Hall

Street. Many later boarded the numerous gaily-decked fishing vessels for a cruise out to Davaar Island and back.

The Council's Entertainment Committee came up with the novel idea of staging floodlit dancing in the late evening on the Quarry Green, which was yet another crowd-puller. Jimmy Shand, the legendary Scottish Country-Dance Bandleader, provided the music at one of the weekly dances and he composed the tune *Campbeltown Cross* to mark his visit.

Before the open-air dancing commenced, local artistes sustained a concert programme on the canopied stage. Our parents sometimes took my two brothers and me along to the early show, which included an interval when members of the audience were asked to participate. Even today, I shiver with embarrassment on recalling the occasion when, at the confident age of 10, I boldly took to the platform and belted out a couple of verses from Alma Cogan's *Sugar in the morning* through a primitive PA system. My elder brother, Robert, bolted and Willie was quietly dumbfounded, but mother and father were, I think rather proud of their middle son that night. As for me, I only did it for the lucrative fee of a small bottle of lemonade, but as the years wore on and I realised that my tone-deaf singing could clear any room, I became more inclined to sympathise with the action Robert took!

A visit to Jack McRobert's hot dog hut further along the promenade before making for home in the twilight via the old railway cutting at Limecraigs usually concluded an enjoyable family excursion.

The annual appearance of travelling fairground shows in Campbeltown during the week prior to the *Glesca Ferr* and for a few weeks thereafter was eagerly anticipated. A funfair of sorts still sets up each year on Kinloch Green but on a much smaller scale.

Older Campbeltonians will recall the names of Jimmy Stringfellow, John Cadona and Randall Taylor, showmen of repute. Stalls and side-shows such as roll-a-penny, pull-the-string and the few 3d or 6d one-armed bandits were, I would contend, much more fun than the expensive ear-piercing electronic mayhem that makes up so much of the modern fairground. Other attractions were the chair-o-planes, swingboats, waltzer, dodgem cars, roundabouts, Wall of Death and a mini Big Dipper described as *The Rib Tickler*. Also included were shooting galleries, darts, Aunt Sally stalls and prize bingo sessions.

Talent contests were sometimes organised at the fairground site, when a stream of young hopefuls dreaming of showbiz stardom took to the stage. Prizes included garish items taken from the shelves of the various stalls and I do not recall anyone making the big time as a result of their Kinloch Green debuts! The showmen's moneybags fairly bulged, though, thanks to the big crowds that usually assembled to watch and pass judgement.

A delicious treat at the conclusion of an organised family outing to the fair was a visit to John McKinlay's nearby fish and chip shop in Saddell Street. A 20-yard queue outside the premises was a common evening occurrence and, without taking anything away from the present chippies in the town, I have never tasted fish and chips with such a distinctive texture and flavour since the business closed on the retirement of Mr McKinlay's son, Douglas some years ago.

Kinloch Green was also the location for occasional visits by a travelling circus and tickets usually sold out weeks in advance. The Big Top was erected on the John Street side of the Green, surrounded by the performers' caravans and the large vehicles that transported the animals.

Other summertime activities on Kinloch Green that drew good crowds of spectators were frequent football matches as teams chased the Campbeltown and District Amateur League championship. There were sometimes three evening games per week, even more if cup fixtures had to be settled, although the finals were held at Kintyre Park. The Kinloch pitch was reserved on the remaining nights or Saturday mornings for the senior and junior boys' football league.

Amateur football in Campbeltown took off in the late fifties, and there were some talented teams on the go then and in the following years including Mayfair Thistle, The Pupils (originally Campbeltown United Amateurs), Lochend, Kinloch Thistle, The Accies, Carradale, Largie and Southend.

The senior boys played either with Glenside, Dalriada, Calton or Kintyre and three of the junior teams I remember were The Wizards, Accies and Rovers.

For film buffs, there were two cinemas operating – The Rex and The Picture House, which was affectionately known as *The Wee Yins*. Thankfully, The Picture House was renovated in recent years and still functions, uniquely, as the oldest working cinema in Scotland.

The renowned Campbeltown Gaelic Choir, under the guidance of legendary conductor M.G. McCallum, won major National Mod trophies regularly and gave performances in the town during the summer. Campbeltown Gaelic Choir recorded much of the background choral music used in the box office film hit, *The Bridal Path*.

The town's licensed premises and cafes enjoyed excellent weeknight trade, a far cry from the subdued atmosphere in evidence today, with two previously busy pubs and a semi-derelict hotel/bar boarded up through lack of business. Sadly, an evening visit to a traditional café in Campbeltown is no longer possible.

For those who preferred some peace and quiet, the hushed surroundings of the Campbeltown Library and Museum provided a relaxing haven, complete silence being guaranteed by the vigilance of caretaker E.P. MacKiernan. The building's interior, though, has been extensively redesigned in recent years, resulting in the scrapping of its exquisitely furnished reading room.

Participation in leisure pursuits certainly did not come to a halt at the conclusion of the summer season. Hundreds of Campbeltown children attended weekly meetings of the various youth movements while many young men and women belonged to organisations such as the Territorial Army, Women's Royal Army Corps, Civil Defence Unit, Royal Observer Corps, or Red Cross. The formerly well maintained building in Bolgam Street, which housed the Civil Defence Unit and Miners' Welfare Club, is now in such a state of dereliction that it could perhaps even be classed as dangerous.

Badminton was an immensely popular game, as was carpet bowling and the leagues were contested vigorously.

Still on sport, there was a winter Junior Football League run by the Campbeltown and District Junior Football Association. The games at Kintyre Park drew attendances that would put some Scottish Football League lower division teams to shame and I was in the ground when a record crowd of more than 3500 spectators watched Campbeltown United in a cup-tie against Loanhead Mayflower in 1958.

The two cinemas opened every night except Sunday, with matinees on Wednesday and Saturday. Bingo was introduced at The Picture House, much to the delight of many housewives (and some men!). Variety shows featuring popular entertainers of the day were sometimes staged in The Rex and were always well attended.

The fabulous 1887-built Victoria Hall, though, was the undoubted entertainment centre of the town. Following its extensive refurbishment, *The Vic* probably enjoyed its finest decade during the swinging sixties, when it was used to its full potential. All kinds of events including concerts, drama festivals, political meetings, produce shows and Christmas Fayres were held there and I remember a radio show hosted by the famous Wilfred Pickles being broadcast in front of a live audience.

But it was as a dance hall that *The Vic* really came into its own. In the fifties, it was the venue for regular dancing by patrons who enjoyed the music of local bands led by Gus McAllister, Joe Morrans or Neil McArthur. Dances in vogue then were *The Swing, Cha-cha, Foxtrot* and *Waltz.* Long forgotten glittering annual occasions such as the Masonic Ball, Kiltie Ball, Black Ball, Police Ball and the Fishermen's Ball also took place in *The Vic.*

When rock'n'roll fever hit Campbeltown, though, sounds of a very different nature bounced from its walls and the music revolution began. The town's young people were quick to learn the intricate steps and movements of jiving, and, although I was still a mere fledgling, I remember my older cousin, Peter Fletcher, telling me about his visit to *The Vic* to hear a Glasgow band called *Ricky Barnes and His All Stars.* Apparently this outfit had two gorgeous female vocalists and the lads showed considerably more interest in the stage show than the local girls, resulting in a preponderance of wallflowers that night!

However, several extremely proficient local rock'n roll partnerships were formed in the hall, including Willie Campbell and Vivienne McGougan; Reggie McManus and Irene Stewart; John McLean and Cathy Robertson; Duncan McGeachy and Isobel Graham. Duncan was particularly good and could easily have become a professional dancer.

The next major change on the musical scene, of course, saw Beatlemania sweeping the world. Beat groups sprung up everywhere in the early sixties and Campbeltown was to produce four that for years afterwards provided the music for the new dance routines.

The original group – and arguably the most polished – was called *Jay and the Zodiacs.* The line up was John Graham (vocalist); Norman Stewart (lead guitarist); Davie Lang (rhythm guitarist);

Andy Muir (bass guitarist); Ian Lang (drums). Later known simply as The Zodiacs, the group released a record in 1967.

Employees at the Andrew Douglas Clothing Factory (now Jaeger) formed another group known as *The Mysterians*, who were very popular for a while. Band members were Jan Mohammed (lead guitarist); Jimmy McNaughton (rhythm guitarist); Stanley Sexton (bass guitarist); James McKinven (drums); Chris Blair (vocalist).

The Sceptres had several combinations before establishing a regular line up. The musicians were Sammy Duncan (lead guitarist); Danny Black (rhythm guitarist); Davie Brodie (bass guitarist); Neil Brodie (drums); Kenny Johnson and Flo McLellan (vocalists).

The fourth group in town were known as *The Regents*, although in the years that followed there were several personnel and name changes. The original members were Calum McAlpine (vocalist); Hinton Craig (lead guitarist and backing vocalist); Brian Linfield (rhythm guitarist); Jimmy McCallum (bass guitarist); Duncan Johnstone (drums).

A former RAF serviceman at the Machrihanish station, Johnny Mullen, was a talented singer/musician and impressionist who performed both with the groups and in some of Campbeltown's pubs. Much of his programme consisted of songs composed by the world famous Jerry Lee Lewis and, like his idol, Johnny accompanied himself with marked enthusiasm on piano.

Dances at *The Vic* regularly attracted crowds of 700-800 people, and the doors were often closed early, which resulted in disappointment for latecomers. The former *Zodiacs* guitarist, Norman Stewart, recalls they heyday of dances admirably when he says that if the crowd was 500 or less he did not feel like playing as he reckoned the atmosphere was not just right. Promoters would be hard pushed to get 200 dancers into *The Vic* nowadays!

Obviously, such a large crowd, especially in exuberant weekend mood, had to be carefully monitored and a well-known team of stewards maintained regular surveillance over the proceedings. Sandy Smith, Henry McGougan, Dan McKinlay, Ivor McKinven, Don Graham and John McLellan punished any unacceptable behaviour with ejection from the hall. The hall-keeper was Morris McSporran, who on his retirement was superseded by John McLean.

The Town Council Entertainment Committee won much praise from the youth of Campbeltown during this era for its enterprise in attracting big names to *The Vic*. Top Glasgow groups, including *Dean Ford and the Gaylords* (later to become internationally known as *The Marmalade*), *The Beatstalkers* and *The Imps* had regular dates in Campbeltown.

Famous names including *Brian Poole and the Tremeloes*, the *Alex Harvey Soul Band*, *Heinz* and *Manfred Mann* all played in the town. Indeed, on the very day that Manfred Mann's blockbuster hit *Doo-Wah-Diddy-Diddy* went to number one in the British charts, the group was performing on stage in none other a place than The Victoria Hall, Campbeltown. Younger readers should note that the aforementioned names easily equalled the adulation showered upon the present day line-ups of *Oasis, The Spice Girls, Boyzone* or *Take That*.

Talented professional Irish Showbands, usually seven strong, became popular at Monday or Wednesday night dances in the hall. Guitars, saxophones, keyboards and drums combined splendidly as the Irishmen expertly played both the hits of the day and old favourites, one frequently requested song being *The Hucklebuck*, a catchy melody that accompanied a dance of the same name.

Younger, but nevertheless every bit as avid dancers – probably better known today as *teenyboppers* – had the opportunity of attending dance teacher Babette Stevenson's junior night on Fridays at her High Street premises. Music was provided, generously, by one of the local groups and Babette's was an ideal stamping ground for novices before they reached an age that permitted entrance to *The Vic*.

The Sunday night youth club in the Christian Institute, run by Councillor Archie McCallum, was also usually packed out with youngsters dancing to live music.

A very different kind of promotion that was guaranteed to fill *The Vic* of an evening was the staging of all-in wrestling shows. Saturday afternoon television coverage of the sport had increased its popularity to a great extent in the UK and tickets sold like wildfire when forthcoming bouts, sometimes featuring celebrities, were advertised. There was one bearded man mountain known as Klondyke Bill who wore a Clydesdale horseshoe on a chain around his neck in place of jewellery. He once ate five platefuls of chips and baked beans and an entire loaf of bread before a show during a brief visit to the Mayfair Café in Main Street!

THE JERKER, MONS HERO, GIANT, GUTTY AND TOOTIE......

Campbeltonians, for some reason, have always imposed nicknames upon one another and the mind boggles at the origin of some of the more puzzling *handles*. A poem documenting a selection of the by-names has been circulating in the town since the 1950's and, as far as I am aware, its composer was none other than Jack McKinven, who is mentioned elsewhere in this book.

There was Pooman and Pelt and Purba and Foals
Stubbles and Sooryins, The Phantom and Coals
Blighty and Beefy, Skins, Mossins and Sticks
Drinks, Ghurka and Scraggs, The Hoodie and Tricks
The Gannet and Shoo Shoo, the Bomber and Gump
Latcher and Comic and Rockall and Stump.

There were wonderful tags such as Whispering Grass
Boorker, Hibs, Chocolate, The Cruban and Brass
Take Weckets and Loafs, Links, Lofty and Lanky
Rabbits, The Whippet, Moose, Peasoup and Stanky
Helpless, and Hopeless and Useless, how droll
Basil, The Waltzer, Samboo, and Toll.

Dannikers, Jonnikers, Jamiekers, Skate
Wisp, Porter, and Bachles, Fog, Pan Cod and Nate
There were other weird tags like Slops, Doink and Dilly
Doopy, Buzz, Sugar and Slingem and Crilly
Then Shullings, Skeenks, Heenga and Nae Soap at A'
Cudgie, Sna' ba', Slaimes, Pluff and Rab Ha'.

Even the dames came in for queer quips
Senorita, London Kate, Snow White, Biscuit Hips
The Blizzard, Bubblin Molly, Apple Sue, Sleepy Annie
Sweetie Bella, Teapoteye and Setturday Sanny
Sarah the Juck, Strings, Smokes and Kate Tarry
Silver Tie, Sailor Jeck, Grozethole, and Take Barry

The Hat and Wee Shavins', Chips, Whitings and Candy
Boorax and Kippers and Nuskas and Handy
Bottleneck and Jamaica and China and Noon
Banana, New Ideas, Crabs, Stirling and Toon
Cuddings and Puddings, Pop, Sockers and Kiltie
Rover, The Hoadler, Creesh, Klondyke and Sheltie.

The Stallion, The Monster, The Clincher and Teepy
Sparra', Jiggs, Glundy and Tidy and Cheery,
Puggie and Nong, Chase, Scout, Flukes and Rootie
The Jerker, Mons Hero, Giant, Gutty and Tootie
The Count, Kubla Khan, and Bunkem and Monkey
Knuckler and Biley and Glaxo and Spunkey.

Glesca Docker, The Bolt, Oliver, Towser and Blabbs
Skulla and Oakie, the Bender and Dabbs
Cullan Dan and Doosan, the Buffalo, The Boar
Bull Montana and Tucker, but there's still many more.

Naturally, some of the marvellous tags held by the persons included
in the poem belonged to kenspeckle characters who were known to
almost everyone in Campbeltown. I have distinct memories of
certain gentlemen who could sometimes change an otherwise
humdrum situation into a very amusing experience, perhaps by their
actions or the deliverance of razor-sharp witticisms. The town
seemed to be well blessed with such individuals in my youth.
There was a chap called Davie Foster, who, strangely enough, did
not possess a nickname, but had an extraordinary fixation for
anything connected with the American Wild West. Many an
imaginary shoot-out we had with him on Kinloch Road, near to his
Park Square home and the middle-aged Davie sometimes galloped
along the road slapping his thigh as if goading some majestic steed
into battle with a band of Red Indian counterparts. His appearance,
though, belied his love of cowboys, as Davie was more often than
not to be seen in a long greatcoat of RAF origin and a skull-tight
leather helmet of the type worn by early aviators.
Davie just could not resist a six-gun duel and, if challenged by us
cruel youngsters he would drop anything he happened to be carrying
to get at his *guns* – often resulting in minor chaos.

Davie lived with his brother, John, also a devotee of J.T.Edson literature, and - as the story goes - on one occasion a police sergeant and constable called to see them on some minor matter. John, after furtively identifying the visitors by slowly opening the creaking door a few inches, called to his brother along the hallway: "Davie, it's the Sheriff an' a deputy. Do ah let them in?"

Another great local character was Jack McKinven - artist, impresario, shopkeeper, amateur filmmaker, entrepreneur, poet and musician. Jack was, indeed, a talented man who had a fondness for American gangster-style clothing, being the owner of some really flash outfits that he wore until an advanced age. With his slicked-back oiled hair and pencil moustache, he really looked the part.

His luxuriantly worded prose which appeared regularly in *The Campbeltown Courier* readers' letters column always caused comment, as did his topical poems.

When he traded as a general merchant from premises in the town's Saddell Street, Jack had a deadly effective method of dealing with bad debtors: he simply put the offending names in the shop window. The overdue accounts were, needless to say, quickly squared up.

He also ran dances and was responsible for organising the *Miss Argyll* contest, an annual parade of beauties from all parts of the county.

Some of Jack's signwriting skills can still be seen in Campbeltown and he painted many fishing boat registration numbers.

He also made some interesting cine films, and I remember seeing a reel based on the antics of American hoodlums, followed by another on a western theme that featured Davie Foster on a Clydesdale horse.

On top of all this, Jack was also the creator of topical cartoons, which were welcomed by successive editors of *The Campbeltown Courier*. As a former editor myself, I was one of many who mourned Jack's passing.

There was also a well-known chap who was bestowed with the apparently uncomplimentary title of *Ducha the Rat*, but this man obtained his nickname following an incident that saw him escape from a sinking ship, thereby saving his skin. He was a street newspaper vendor and could be seen nightly at *Cook's Corner*, the junction of Main Street and Longrow South, selling the Glasgow evening papers. *Ducha*, whose real name was Duncan McKinlay, applied a unique pronunciation to one of his titles, the *Evening*

Citizen, and he laudably urged passers-by to pick up a copy of the "Shitayezinn."

Many townspeople will remember another grand character with the baptismal name of George Muir, but everyone in Campbeltown knew him as *Geordie*.

Geordie worked for years with Andrew McMillan on his smallholding beside Kilkerran Cemetery and his favourite pastime was fishing for mackerel off the Old Quay. *Geordie's* simple rig was a long length of thick bamboo cane of considerable vintage, a basic reel that held a length of nylon gut line and six feathered hooks weighted with an old steel bolt. It was, nonetheless, used with remarkable success.

Many aspiring sea anglers equipped with expensive fibreglass rods, complicated running gear and elaborate spinners had cause to look on with envy as *Geordie* pulled in the mackerel with little apparent effort.

He sometimes asked the person responsible for playing the dance music on the Old Quay to put on *Scotland the Brave*, by Jimmy Shand, claiming that the mackerel were attracted to the harbour area by the tune.

Following the death of his mother, *Geordie* spent his twilight years in the tender care of the nursing staff of the former Witchburn Hospital, Campbeltown.

Sandy Townsley, or *Scoot*, as he was called, belonged to the noted tinker family of that name. He used to tour the housing estates with a sack over his shoulder while one-handedly playing the mouth organ. *Scoot* had a slight deformity that caused him to adopt a hirpling gait, and, dressed in long overcoat, he was a conspicuous figure indeed. He was well aware of the households that were sympathetic to his cause and he executed his tactics accordingly by marching back and forth in front of the various sitting room windows until his reward of a few pennies or a snack was forthcoming.

The effects of too much alcohol, as opposed to the onset of eccentricity, caused a number of men to fall into the *character* category. Obviously, in my younger days I was slightly confused by the regular groggy antics of certain Campbeltown individuals. As time went on, however, I realised that excessive worshipping of the God Bacchus was responsible for their erratic behaviour and that, indeed, it allowed a form of escape from seemingly unsurpassable situations which had been allowed to develop.

I remember one man who was a former school dux and football *keepie-uppie* expert, but it would be unfair to name him. He spent his latter years on the dole, doing occasional casual work on the Old Quay when the puffers called with cargo or in Donald Shaw's coal yard in Kinloch Road. He invariably converted his hard-earned wages into that popular fortified nectar the 50's and 60's - an alluring concoction with the obscure brand name of VP Wine. But instead of laughing at this man on my frequent *doon the quay* excursions, I learned to laugh with him and the pearls of wisdom that he sometimes uttered forth were perfect examples of a formidable brain gone to waste. One of his favourite and oft-used expressions was: "Never tell a lie, Scottie."

Two other men employed by Donald Shaw on a coal delivery round also came into the *character* bracket. They were Willie Gilchrist and Erchie Bell, known affectionately as *Basil* and *Ding-a-ling. Ding-a-ling* was the driver of the yellow Bedford lorry and *Basil* rode shotgun. The women on the round used to say that *Basil*, with his rugged swarthy looks, could "charm the birds off a tree" and *Ding-a-ling* was never stumped for a witty riposte.

The two pals were known to take a refreshment and one well-recounted story involving the pair stemmed from an occasion that saw them carrying out a bulk delivery to a farm on the Campbeltown-Southend road. On approaching the farm road-end, a young police constable raised his arm in an official manner and stopped the lorry with the words: "I'm sorry, you can't come in here. We've got a case of anthrax."

Ding-a-ling responded instantly: "Don't worry, son, we'll drink anything," a reply which became legend in Campbeltown and has caused many a chuckle!

The passing of my friend Charlie Farmer (*Feenie*), was also much lamented in Campbeltown. Ex-miner *Feenie*, who was an accomplished soccer player in his youth, was latterly employed on the Council refuse wagon and his stentorian renderings of Mario Lanza songs brightened up many a housewife's day. His witticisms also generated much mirth in Campbeltown.

There was an occasion when, during one of my many pavement chats with *Feenie*, an aged former local Grammar School teacher bade us a friendly "good afternoon." As he walked on, I remarked that the man must be of considerable vintage, to which I received a typical *Feenie* reply: "Owld? That man can mind when Ben Ghulean wis a chuckie stone!"

There is a story told that concerns *Feenie* and a pint of beer. It appears that one night in the Kinloch Bar in Main Street, he noticed that each time he came back from a visit to the gents the level of his ale was considerably lower, which suggested that someone was having a fly swig during his absence. In an attempt to put a stop to the beer thievery, *Feenie* asked the barman for pen and paper and, having reduced the level of a fresh pint by a couple of inches, left a note beside the glass before making another visit to the lavatory. The message stated – quite erroneously -: 'I spat in this pint'.

Feenie was devastated on his return to the bar counter to discover that someone had added a few scrawled words that read: 'So did I!'

Characters could be found in the fishing fleet as well and one noteworthy individual was Andy McSporran, who was referred to by many in Campbeltown and beyond as *Spotchie*.

Several fishing-related songs still sung locally, including *The Herring Blues, The tides they are a changin'* and *Machrie Bay* were written by Jim Brodie and the ebullient *Spotchie*. He was also the instigator of many an onboard practical joke at the herring ring net fishing.

On one occasion, whilst serving as a crewman on the *Fiona* (CN 165), *Spotchie* and his shipmates were crossing the Minch, bound for Mallaig to land the herring they had caught off Barra. The boat's skipper, the late Peter McKinlay, told me the story a long time ago of how *Spotchie* laid a bet with his shipmates that he could conceal himself in such a way that his hiding place would not be discovered. The other fishermen reckoned they were on a winner; after all, the possibilities open to *Spotchie* on a 55-foot ring netter were limited, although it was dark at the time, but an intensive search of every nook and cranny on the vessel proved fruitless. His mates began to wonder if something sinister had happened and were on the point of raising a general alarm when *Spotchie* revealed himself. He was straddling the boat's bow on the outside of the hull, hanging on to the stemhead by little more than his fingertips, as the *Fiona* sliced through the waves.

Sadly, *Spotchie*, aged only 33,was to die a few years later in a tragic accident on board a fishing vessel moored in Campbeltown Harbour. One story I like recounting concerns another seafarer, Charlie Robertson, who was known in Campbeltown as *Fog*. The herring fleet had largely departed for *The North* fishing, but skipper Charlie was short of crewmen. When he signed on at the Labour Exchange, the spinster clerkess asked him why he was not at sea, to which he replied: "Och, I canna get men."

"Men!" she expostulated, "*I'll* soon get you men!"

"Aweh, wumman, sure ye canna get wan for yerself," was the instant reply that has become folklore in Campbeltown fishing circles.

There were several retired Campbeltown fisherman who were characters in their own right and I often listened spellbound to their yarns of bumper herring catches and heroic maritime deeds, though as time went on I was to doubt the authenticity of some of the tales! My favourite storytellers were Andrew (*Bomber*) Brown, Duncan (*Captain*) Wilkinson, and David (*Teedultie*) McLean. The only props required for this particular form of theatre were a decent sized poke of their favourite sweeties, an upturned herring box and a convenient mooring bollard.

Yes, there is no doubt that the aforementioned gentlemen and, of course, many more, all played a part in making the Campbeltown of that era an interesting place to live in.

PART TWO

GROWING UP IN CAMPBELTOWN

EARLY DAYS

Apparently, the glorious dawn that broke over 4 John Street,
Campbeltown, on May 3, 1950, its peace interrupted almost
imperceptibly by the soft twittering of songbirds, was a particularly
pleasant sight. However, around 90 minutes later, the early morning
tranquillity was shattered by the unmistakable cry of a newly born
baby boy letting everyone know he had entered the world. I had
upset my mother's plans to check in at Craigard Maternity Hospital a
couple of days later by arriving ahead of schedule, something I wish
I was as good at nowadays! Unfortunately for my parents, the
wailing was to continue for the next 12 months as I progressed
through the first year of life. My father toiled at night as a herring
ring net fisherman and I am told his sleep was interrupted constantly
whilst trying to rest during the day.

Home was a room and kitchen with an outside toilet, part of the
housing block that sits between the Scout Hall and Benmhor. It was
renovated a long time ago to create several larger, well found private
flats.

In 1950, though, things were different. The western end of John
Street at that time supported a friendly, tight little community of 11
families on two floors. My elder brother, Robert, was 18-months-old
when I was born, and younger brother, Willie, was to come along
three years later, creating a pressing need for larger accommodation.
Before that happened, however, life continued happily in the
Benmhor area and my earliest memories are from this period.

Strangely enough, I can remember all the tenants, although I had not
quite attained four years of age when we moved house - along with
six of the other families - to the Meadows Estate. Our near
neighbours included close family; my grandparents on the Gillies
side lived next door and, a few yards along the backcourt at the top
of a stone stairway, was the home of Uncle Hughie and Auntie
Martha Fletcher.

Washing was done in a communal washhouse, where fires were lit to
heat the water that filled big cast iron tubs. It must have been
backbreaking work for my mother when I consider the amount of
laundry – including soiled nappies and my father's fishing clothes –

she had to wash by hand, her only aid being a primitive scrubbing board.

My earliest buddy, John Finn, lived with his parents next door to my Auntie Martha and he called me *Faiffie* for some reason. Our favourite game was playing with a big blue pedal car, which was under the shared ownership of Robert and me. Hours were spent taking turns at driving or pushing this wonderful toy that was based on the Austin of England model.

I made frequent visits to the home of bachelor skipper Geordie Thomson and his spinster sister, Mary Alice, who lived directly above us. Geordie was master on the whisky puffer, *Pibroch*, and he sometimes took us over to the Old Quay to board the vessel when she was in port.

The house next door to Geordie and Mary Alice, on the same landing, was another favourite port of call. Here lived a wonderfully kind silver-haired old lady with completely unlined features and whom everyone knew as *Kendrick*, a shortened version of Mrs. McKendrick. She still had a massive black kitchen range for heating the house and on which she did some cooking, though there was a little gas cooker in the room as well; the big kitchen also had a curtained-off set in bed. *Kendrick* had a special biscuit tin that held treats for me and other youthful callers and I have happy memories of sitting by the spotless black-leaded range, the brightly polished brass poker and tongs glinting beside the blazing fire while I munched shortbread and listened to her stories.

The Auld Scots Dictionary contains the word *throwther*, meaning helter-skelter; in confusion. It is the nearest in spelling and meaning I can match to my mother's favoured description of my periodic mischievous behaviour while I was still a tot. The evidently corrupted word she and others used was *throoither*, but I think either would have suited when I think of some of the capers I was involved in.

My mother had just acquired a brand new electric iron as a replacement for the ancient smoothing iron she previously used. I thought that the boat-like shape of this avant-garde household gadget would enable it to float like all the similarly designed vessels we played with in the big zinc tub on bath night. My mother was next door in granny's house when I decided to conduct an experiment, which I know now to be based on the Principle of Archimedes. I filled the deep kitchen sink to the brim, gingerly placed the iron on the water and watched uncomprehendingly as it sank rapidly to the bottom, trailing the flex and plug behind it!

Another aquatic incident also involved Robert, but I have been assured through the years that I was the instigator. Again, it was boat-orientated and I am led to understand that I convinced my elder brother that our craft would sail on the kitchen carpet if there was enough water to float them. With mother once more preoccupied, the sink was plugged, filled and allowed to run over at will. It is just as well that we lived on the ground floor!

My grandfather, Bob, drove one of the former Argyll County Council road maintenance lorries and, I think in order to give my mother some respite, he occasionally took me with him in the vehicle, usually to Killellan Quarry, near Southend. The roadmen in those days brewed their break-time tea in billycans over small open fires that were lit on the roadside verges wherever they happened to be working. After one trip in the lorry, incidentally during which I accidentally broke one of its headlamps, I described the tea-making procedure in detail to Robert. The following morning at the crack of dawn, we got up before the household awoke and decided to have a go at brewing tea. Using pages from my mother's prized cookery book as fuel and matches from the gas cooker for ignition, we lit a small fire on the kitchen floor. Even today I shudder to think of the disastrous consequences which could have occurred had it not been for the fact that our Auntie Catherine was staying over and she awoke just in time to realise what was happening.

The Simpson family occupied one of the John Street houses, at the gable end beside the Scout Hall. Mr and Mrs Simpson had three sons, Archie and twins George and Jimmy. Although the twins were slightly older than we were, age did not matter when games were being played, and everyone joined in. We were pretty well off for toys but on one occasion Robert decided to take the kitchen fire poker outside as a plaything and the inevitable happened; Jimmy received an accidental blow. In tears, he reported the assault to my mother who made recompense with an orange and a silver sixpence - fair compensation in the austere days of immediate post war Britain. Robert was taken indoors as punishment and it was he who answered a knock on the door shortly afterwards to find Jimmy's twin brother, George, standing on the step. He was armed with a club-like piece of wood, which he handed to Robert and requested, in a slightly lisping voice: "Hit me, Lobert!" Fortunately my mother prevented any further violence occurring and saved herself sixpence and another orange!

In common with many other married women in Campbeltown, my Granny Gillies was widely known by her maiden name of Annie Ralston, locally pronounced *Raahlston*. She was a formidable character of the old school and did not suffer fools gladly but at the same time had a heart of gold. Her qualities were fully personified one summer evening when a slightly tipsy sailor from a visiting submarine decided to help himself to her beloved cat called Gilles, pronounced *Jeelus*. Intelligence reached her at John Street that the matelot had been seen passing the fairground on Kinloch Green, making for the harbour with Gilles cradled in his arms. Granny donned her traditional rig of black hat and coat and marched to the New Quay, where she shrugged off the approaches of the gangway duty rating, boarded the vessel and demanded to see the captain instantly. Gilles was restored to the comforts of home 10 minutes later.

When Willie was born in August 1953, the need for more spacious living quarters became a matter of urgency but it was not until eight months later, in March 1954, that my parents were given the keys to a brand new home at 175 Ralston Road. The attractive semi-detached houses were being built by the Scottish Special Housing Association in conjunction with Campbeltown Town Council and allocations were made as each building was completed, in our case two days after the last brushful of paint had been applied to the front door.

The flitting was accomplished over two evenings and the furniture was carried in a big yellow Hydro Electric Board Ford van driven by another uncle, Duncan Colville, who was a Board employee.

The house, built among the rolling fields of Meadows Farm at the top end of Ralston Road, was a revelation after the cramped urban quarters of John Street. My mother marvelled at the modern electric cooker in the kitchenette, complete with a hotplate for making scones and pancakes, a big electric boiler that would take so much of the strain out of washday and the indoor coal cellar. The spacious bedrooms and bathroom, front and back doors and large garden added to my parents' joy. They were to remain there, where they made improvements over the years and kept a fine garden, until they passed on while still in middle age, mother in 1973 and father in 1976.

Today, in 2000, there are still a few of the original tenants in residence, though many of the houses are now under private ownership. I note, however, with pleasure on my occasional visits to the place of my upbringing that the area has been looked after to a very high standard.

RALSTON ROAD

I spent my fourth birthday nursing a bandaged head. The injury was caused when I fell against a cement mixer, and was one of many bumps and scratches sustained by me during construction work as contractors endeavoured to complete the house building programme and tarmacadam Ralston Road's final 250 yards to the point where it met Tomaig Road.

Divine days were spent at play on the building site; after all, the attraction of sand, water, mud and cement, coupled with a band of good natured and tolerant workmen made the place pretty well irresistible to Robert, myself and a few other children. Despite the fact that we always finished the day in a muckier state than any navvy, I suspect my mother was secretly delighted that our boundless energy was being expended outdoors, leaving her in peace to look after the infant Willie and the house.

Ralston Road was completed not long afterwards and, as in John Street, the neighbours in our *bit* lived in harmony. The immediate area was tenanted by a true cross-section of the community including a distillery worker, office workers, fishermen, miners, a bank teller, headmaster, GPO engineer, barman and insurance agent. Everyone in the vicinity was in employment, which was just as well since the majority of the householders had young growing families.

To this day, when I meet former residents of the top end of Ralston Road, the conversation invariably refers to the happy times spent there. While there was certainly no abject poverty, nobody was wealthy either; the riches came from the quality of life enjoyed and the modern *Neighbours from Hell* situation, so common now, was a complete nonentity.

Our first through-the-wall neighbours were the Stark family headed by Jimmy, a miner who had come from Loanhead to work at Machrihanish, though the house was occupied afterwards by John and Sheila McLachlan, followed by Charlie and Sandra Campbell, two young local couples of whom my mother was particularly fond. My first Ralston Road pal, Don McIvor and his sister, Anne, lived over the fence at number 177 with their young widowed mother. They were to move around two years later in an exchange of houses with our long-term neighbours, Mr and Mrs Charles Hastie, whose sons, David and Kenneth, became part of the ever-growing band of youngsters in the locality. Another early friend was Charles Jonson, who stayed at number 179; his father was a Norwegian construction worker called Elif. I made more and more friends and before my schooldays could be found in the company of Brian Warren, Graham Morrison, Jim McIntyre, William Gillies (no relation), Stewart McLean and Tom McFarlane.

I have gin clear memories of my first day at school in the *Wee Grammar* on August 23, 1955. My mother took me there at the appointed hour, wearing an obviously fashionable coat in a greenish colour that had big checks and pronounced buttoned sleeve cuffs. Seemingly I was mustard keen to get into school, unlike some of my counterparts from the Meadows area, and there were lots of tears spilled, particularly by some of the little girls who lived nearby. However, nearly half a century later, I have absolutely no intention of embarrassing them by revealing identities, although I can even remember what one of them was wearing that day!

My primary one teacher was the middle-aged Miss Mary McConnachie, of the hotel and bus company family, a firm believer in the *three R's* principle. Miss Mary McMillan pursued a similar teaching policy as the primary two mistress. I must have shone academically because I was placed first in class during both years and I still have the book prizes awarded to me.

On then, to Millknowe, and the primary three class of Miss Huntly Smith. The school's headmaster was another Ralston Road resident, William Beveridge, who lived at number 168.

A. & P. McConnachie ran special school buses - in the morning, lunchtime and at the school closing time of four o'clock. The fare was 2d, and I generally used the service if the weather was inclement, when discipline was maintained in the packed bus by the presence of Mr Beveridge in his reserved seat. However, in fine weather, I ran like a hare to school via Tomaig Road, Witchburn Road and the bonded warehouse-lined Glebe Street, stopping only briefly at Alastair McConnachie's Big Kiln shop to trade my bus fare for two big penny caramels or some similar dainties.

The homeward trek in good weather took longer, when my progress was punctuated by stops to talk to the whisky warehousemen in Glebe Street or at the Unigate Creamery to watch workers steam-cleaning the big milk churns that had been emptied into huge cheese-making vats earlier in the day.

On sunny summer days, I paused often at the Witch Burn, over which Tomaig Road crosses. This stream was also known as *The Shaachel Burn*, and its reeds provided excellent cover for many little minnows and sticklebacks, which I caught easily with cupped hands. Unlike now, when most youngsters spend lots of time indoors playing with computer games or other electronic gadgetry, weekends or school holidays found us outside from early morning; we had neither playing field or swing park, nor did we need them.

Stormy weather, however, meant frustrating periods of confinement to the house, and time spent playing with toys – mainly Dinky or Corgi vehicles – or taking part in board games such as snakes and ladders, ludo or tiddlywinks, in the days when the number of television sets in Ralston Road could be counted on one hand. When conditions were fine, though, happy hours were spent at play with immediate neighbours including Graham Morrison, the Hastie boys, William and Jim Gillies, Jim McIntyre and John McWhirter on *the railway*, which was the former track of the Campbeltown and Machrihanish Light Railway Company's train to Machrihanish. The service was discontinued in the 1930's but, twenty odd years later, parts of the rails and sleepers of the narrow gauge line could still be seen only feet from our back garden fence. Imaginative use of discarded household items such as bed frames, old rugs and cardboard boxes led to the assembly of mysterious forts, admittance to which was only guaranteed if membership of the secret society currently in fashion had been obtained.

Another favourite playing area was *Taddie Loch*, a little reed-bound lochan behind Ralston Road and adjacent to Bluebell Wood (now the site of the Kintyre Gardens private housing estate) that fairly abounded with tadpoles and newts, hence its name. Further up towards Crosshill Farm was *The Big Slide*, a steep earthen hillside scar caused by soil erosion. Sliding down its length on a makeshift sled of hardboard or cardboard was a particular delight. Mothers were anything but delighted with the consequences of an accidental tumble, which resulted in clothes being caked in clay.

Westward exploration of the railway, where it ran through a mini cutting, led to further friendships with boys from the top end of Tomaig Road and the far end of Crosshill Avenue until eventually there was a gang of more than 20 lads of varying ages on the go. I use the *gang* description loosely, since there were certainly no sinister tendencies shown, and older boys looked after the more youthful members with patient tolerance and acceptance.

Some of my Tomaig friends were Alex and Roddie Girvan, Donald McKinven, Douglas and Ian McArthur and Sandy McCallum. Ian Forshaw and Douglas McCallum were my Crosshill buddies. A few of the boys had pet dogs – I remember Bronco and Rouguie – and I pestered the life out of my mother by continually pleading for a *doag* of my own. But she had a strange aversion to dogs and cats and my persistent harassment met with an unwavering refusal to negotiate.

The gang's meeting place was on the vacant ground beside the last house in Tomaig Road, which was tenanted by police sergeant Dougie Crawford, a gentleman who commanded our complete respect! Initially I regarded Dougie with awe, but as I got to know him better I found him to be a very interesting man and I occasionally helped him with DIY work in the big garage/shed beside his house.

Sometimes we followed the old railway line to a smallholding called The Flush, midway between Campbeltown and Stewarton. The farmer's name was Donald McDonald, hence his nickname of *Donald Twice*.

The Episcopalian Church graveyard set in the hillside on the road leading to the farms of Crosshill, Narrowfield and Tomaig, was another favourite haunt. I may say that the graveyard's popularity stemmed from the attraction of the easily climbed trees, and not because of any interest in the macabre.

Further towards Bengullion, directly below Narrowfield Farm, is a dense little valley of trees and bushes that we called *Currie's Glen*, named after the then resident farmer. The glen was teeming with wildlife and we gained considerable knowledge of the workings of Mother Nature there. Mrs Currie was a kindly person who was genuinely interested in our comings and goings and it was she who introduced us to the Country Code, carefully explaining the do's and don'ts. Mrs Currie also sold fresh eggs and home produced honey to my mother and other housewives in Ralston Road.

There were three other farms in the Tomaig area, occupied by Duncan McCallum, Willie Hamilton and Dougie McKendrick. We became well known to them thanks to regular excursions into the depths of the extensive Tomaig Glen, on the lower slopes of Bengullion. In high summer, our hot bodies were cooled by a quick dip in the crystal waters of an icy waterfall-fed pool in the glen. Although we were all well fed children, hunger was never far away during the hill climbing expeditions and a favourite way of alleviating this was by the surreptitious removal of a juicy turnip from one of the fields. Someone always had a knife and the spoils were peeled and shared equally. On other occasions, potatoes and onions that had been deftly purloined from the kitchen vegetable basket were roasted in the glowing embers of a dying wood fire and eaten with relish.

Another dubious source of nourishment came from *sooracks* and *sheepie-mehs*, a colourful description for two types of clover that gave out strange tasting juices when sucked, the consumption of which appears not to have done us any harm.

Games including football, *rats and rabbits*, *aleevo* and *beds* were played under streetlights on the tarmac of Ralston Road in the late afternoon and evening darkness of winter months. *Kick-the-can* was introduced by Anne Moffat and her brother, Alastair, when they moved to Ralston Road from Glasgow on their father's appointment as manager of the local clothing factory. My interest in football by this time was becoming intense, and regular unofficial games were organised at High Kintyre Park on Saturdays.

The energy for such after school activities – on the Gillies brothers part at any rate– was provided by the consumption of thick slices of bread spread liberally with jam; sometimes we shared the greater part of a loaf before teatime! I have mouth-watering recollections of the delicious combination of new, soft plain bread smeared with spoonfuls of rhubarb and ginger jam. My mother, like many of her contemporaries of the time, was a firm believer in preparing a substantial midday meal, usually preceded by steaming bowls of home-made soup, followed by a light high tea in the evening, and the pieces served as ideal top-up sustenance. I am sure that my ability to eat almost anything that is put in front of me comes from those early days, when, to satisfy a voracious appetite generated by healthy outdoor pursuits, nothing was ever left on my plate.

The street games were seldom interrupted by passing traffic, since there were few cars to be seen in Ralston Road, unlike today's unbroken line of parked vehicles that stretches its entire length. In fact, there is a point in time when I do not recollect any more than six cars and two motor cycles over a distance of 500 yards. Jack McRobert, the shopkeeper, had a light blue Riley Pathfinder (RSM 835). Ian Taylor, an insurance agent drove a Ford and landscape gardener Malcolm Harvey owned a huge blue/black Morris (AGA 881) that was always left on the Ralston Road slope for easy bump starting in the morning. John Warren, a bank teller, had a black Ford Popular (732 MPH) and his neighbour, insurance agent John Morrison was later to acquire one of the first Minis in the town when his beige Ford Consul was traded in. John Scott, an agricultural officer, was the owner of a black Triumph Mayflower, a distinctive car with angular lines. Little did anyone realise then that this model, along with the later Triumph Herald, would eventually become rare collector's items worth many times their original value.

The motor bikes belonged to barman Eddie McKinven, who had a grey BSA Bantam, and farmworker Gavin Muir rode a much larger black machine on his daily runs into the countryside.

It was around this time that my brother Willie and his pal, Neil Thomson, caused a minor panic by performing a disappearing act when they went missing for hours. It was finally established that the intrepid pair of five-year-olds had completed the 10-mile round trip to Machrihanish on their pedal tricycles, a journey obviously made easier by the scarcity of traffic and not an idea even to be contemplated today. On his return, Willie complained of a sore bottom and I think he was saved from further discomfort in that region only because my mother was intensely relieved that he was safe and well.

Apart from the service buses, the only other regular traffic to be seen in Ralston Road during the first few years were the vans belonging to various traders.

The first travelling shop I encountered was actually a horse-drawn affair owned by Jock Girvan. He sold greengroceries and other bits and pieces from a brightly painted covered wagon with green tarpaulin sides. It was pulled by a beautiful white horse and I will never forget Jock's laconic reply when I asked him one sunny Saturday afternoon if I could buy anything with the old halfpenny I had in my pocket (one fifth of 1p!).

"Ye can have a clap at the horse son," he said.

Both the McGeachy and Kerr butcher vans visited the street twice per week. A youthful Malcolm O'May, who now works in the Tesco supermarket, drove for Kerr and was definitely the housewives' favourite. His complimentary comments and patter fairly attracted the women to his van and one of his one-liners on describing a cut of meat was: "There you are my dear – tender as your heart!"
If I happened to be in the van with my mother, Malcolm sometimes asked me about my football allegiance and if I said I followed Glasgow Rangers, a few extra link sausages were quickly added to the meat parcel!
Campbeltown's first ice-cream van belonged to Jack and Jessie McRobert, who lived at number 155 Ralston Road. They also sold sweets from the hallway of their house before planning permission was obtained to build the *The Wee Shop* on a vacant lot adjacent to the Council rent office further down the street. A particular delicacy was Jessie's toffee apples.
The ice-cream van was a small Austin in a livery of light blue and yellow with a pronounced hump at the rear of the driving compartment, which enabled the vendor to stand upright. To me, it resembled a snail carrying its shell and was a familiar sight for a long time in the streets of the town as well as at sports days and other public events. The McRoberts later acquired two mobile shops that plied locally and around the countryside.
Other vehicles that traded during the fifties and sixties in Ralston Road belonged to Jimmy Thomson, fishmonger; Lipton the grocer; Charlie Webster, grocer; R.J. MacKay, grocer; the SCWS, who had bakery and grocery vans on the road, and a fish and chip van. The well-known Lanarkshire bakery firm, Dalziel, actually sent a maroon-painted Ford van loaded with cellophane wrapped rolls to sell in the town and Ralston Road was one of the places visited, always in the evening. When the driver made his regular stops, an assistant shouted: "Dazell's Roh-ells."

*

Sunday mornings were strictly reserved for attendance at Castlehill Church and Sunday school, followed by a traditional Sunday lunch. One year, I was chosen to read the lesson at the Sunday school prize-giving service in the church and my mother bought me a new short trousered suit for the occasion. On the Saturday I was sent to Dan Morrison's barber shop for a neat trim - the final touch that would ensure a smartly turned-out boy next morning. I had other ideas, however, and asked Dan's assistant, Charlie McFadyen, to give me a crew cut, the popular ultra-short American style that was becoming fashionable in Britain at the time. When I arrived home, mother took one look at my shorn cranium, which highlighted the white scars of past head wounds, and almost passed out!

On a similar theme, I could easily have been sent home from church in disgrace one Sunday morning had it not been for the fact that a handkerchief stuffed into my mouth prevented me from exploding with laughter. On the day in question, my father decided that Willie's hair, which was seen to be overlapping his ear, needed shortening slightly. He decided, therefore, to perform a minimal emergency hair cutting operation, which would suffice until Willie could be sent to Dan's salon the following day. The results of his endeavours, however, left Willie in need of immediate remedial treatment, which was impossible, of course, on a Sunday. I only had to glance at the direction of his right ear to be overcome with the desire to burst forth with uncontrollable mirth.

The Sunday school summer picnic and Christmas party were two dates eagerly looked forward to on our social calendar. The party was held in the hall in Lochend Street used by Castlehill Church and involved lots of goodies, games and a present from Santa. During the summer holidays, two West Coast Motors buses bedecked with streamers were used to transport the children to beaches at Carradale, or perhaps Southend, Macharioch or Dalkeith (near Glenbarr) for the annual picnic.

An exciting summer event organised for children was the Miners' Gala Day. In the weeks leading up to this thrilling occasion I always developed a close friendship with a miner's son, in the hope that one of a limited number of spare tickets would find its way to me. I was lucky twice and really enjoyed the outings, again at beach locations. One day out - albeit a long one – that was anticipated keenly was the special sailing to Ayr on the T.S. *Duchess of Hamilton*, which was run for the benefit of local farmers wishing to attend the Ayrshire Agricultural Society's annual May show. The show date coincided with a school holiday and my mother took the opportunity of browsing through the big shops of Ayr while we youngsters spent carefully hoarded funds on new toys. On the return journey a high tea, which consisted of a main course followed by by cakes, scones and biscuits, was served on white linen cloths that covered immaculate silver service laid tables. Lighter snacks could also be had in the vessel's cafeteria and the bar did a roaring trade with punters who had ostensibly gone below decks to look at the engines!

Family vacations presented a slight problem for my mother, since the fishing industry *cleaning time* in late spring was a leisurely affair that extended to a period of weeks, and it was generally accepted by all concerned that crew holidays were incorporated in the time off. The boats were all back at sea when the school breaks came round and this meant that my father was unable to join us.

We had some great holidays organised by mother, though, at various locations in Ayrshire, Dumfriesshire and Lanarkshire, as guests of her sister, Agnes, and gamekeeper husband Willie Stevenson. Visits were made, also, to my Auntie Cathie and Uncle Dan when they lived in the Glasgow area. One of their early homes in the city was at Garrioch Crescent, in the West End, and it was during a holiday there that I experienced my one and only trip on a rattling Glasgow tramcar and rode the underground for the first time. I had also never before seen morning rolls being bought already spread with butter or cheese. I was intrigued by this early morning transaction, which I witnessed whilst queuing for fresh milk in a little dairy nearby. Another red letter day was on October 31, when Ralston Road in the post teatime darkness came alive with the appearance of witches, pirates, ghosts and other heavily disguised weird characters carrying candlelit lamps made from hollowed out turnips. The occasion, of course, was Halloween and visits to neighbouring houses culminated in a healthy catch of apples and nuts. Some households organised parties, where *dooking* for apples and other Halloween activities took place.

A few days later, on November 5, bonfire night was held to commemorate Guy Fawkes' failed attempt to blow up the Houses of Parliament. For weeks beforehand, householders were pestered almost daily for old newspapers, packing, empty boxes; indeed anything that would fuel a fire. The cache was kept under cover in the field bordering Ralston Road until the big night arrived, when the collected material was built up into a tepee-shaped structure. Everyone had a supply of fireworks and, against the background glow generated by the huge fire, a colourful display lit up the area.

I looked forward to the traditional festivals of Christmas and New Year with particular relish, although Yuletide celebrations in Campbeltown then were definitely overshadowed by the observance of Hogmanay – a trend that has now been reversed. I can never remember being disappointed on Christmas morning, however, and when I think of those breathtaking crack of dawn discoveries I shared with Robert and Willie, it comes home to me that my parents must have made real sacrifices at that time of year in order to fulfil our dreams.

While turkey for Christmas dinner is now the norm, it was quite uncommon then in our wee corner of Caledonia. The fare usually consisted of soup made with a big plump hen that served as the centrepiece of the main course, served with a variety of vegetables and roast potatoes. Dessert was either the ubiquitous Christmas pudding or one of my mother's homebaked chocolate gateaux with thick cream. And, of course, there were fruit and sweets in abundance.

Older people, especially my Carradale Granny Brownie, invariably treated the New Year holiday much more seriously and she made immaculate preparations during the week between Christmas and Hogmanay. My father usually collected his supply of whisky, beer, sherry, port, Babycham and Advocaat a few days in advance; he had a preference for Vat 69 whisky, which came in a quaintly shaped black bottle.

A traditional evening meal of home cured salt herring and potatoes, a repast savoured by my parents but one which took me a long time to develop a taste for, was served perhaps twice during the last few days of the old year.

One of my duties was to hand in a huge enamel pie dish to David Kerr's butcher shop in Main Street. Kerr and the bakery firm of John Hoyne next door worked together to produce delicious steak pies, the like of which I have never eaten since. The owner's name was marked on each dish in indelible ink and Hogmanay in Kerr's shop was a scene of bedlam as hordes of customers turned up to collect their orders.

My father also performed an annual ritual each Hogmanay night at around nine o'clock when the ashes in the living room coal fire were raked out and taken outside to the bin. We were packed off to bed early so that my parents could dress up in their best clothes - another tradition they observed annually.

There were never any riotous parties held in our house. New Year was a fairly dignified affair involving visits from neighbours and relatives and my parents generally went to bed around 3am.

After breakfast on New Years morning, we children called at the surrounding houses to offer New Year greetings and were rewarded with small glasses of ginger or raspberry wine and slabs of shortbread. We laughed at the staggering figures of some of the more enthusiastic revellers making for home in mid-morning.

The Kerr/Hoyne gastronomic delight, accompanied by fluffy mashed potatoes and winter vegetables, graced the New Years Day dinner table. The meal started with big platefuls of broth and pudding consisted of helpings of homemade trifle.

The afternoon of New Years Day meant a family outing to the Campbeltown Ornithological Society's annual bird show in the Drill Hall, where the air was filled with the calls of cagebirds, cockerels, bantams, hens and pigeons, followed by visits to more friends and relatives who lived further afield.

*

When I was seven, the Clyde herring fishing industry suffered a serious slump and this development forced my father and many of his friends to give up their chosen calling. Along with a number of other Campbeltown and Carradale fishermen, he found employment with a tug company called Steel and Bennie in far off Greenock, where he served on the *Meteor*. He later joined the Clyde Port Authority's fleet in Glasgow, sailing on the *Flying Duck*.

This provided financial stability for my mother, but the geographical location of the Upper Clyde and my father's work pattern meant that he could only manage home occasionally on Saturdays aboard the steamer *Duchess of Hamilton*, returning upriver on the same day, though he was allowed some weekends off.

I was glad he was on the tugs that year as it meant evening visits to me in Ward 10 of Glasgow's Southern General Hospital, where I had been admitted for an operation to have my tonsils removed. I was one of a busload of around 30 Campbeltown children, all suffering from a similar throat complaint. It was my first time away from home and I marvelled at the city sights, especially the trolley buses and noisy tramcars.

The herring shoals were still largely eluding the fishermen when my father joined the construction firm of Tarmac, who were involved in the extensive refurbishment of RAF Machrihanish. He was employed there as a timekeeper and was glad to be working at home once more. I rose at six o'clock on many mornings, Sundays excepted, to collect rolls for his packed lunch from Hoyne's bakery so that my mother could make them up in time for his 7am departure. I was suitably rewarded for my efforts when I was given a marvellous football that I played with for years afterwards.

As with most fishermen unavoidably confined to shore, my father hankered after the sea and he sorely missed the maritime life. Nobody was surprised when he went back to the fishing on Tarmac's departure from the area, although results were fairly erratic and my mother's qualities as a good manager were fully utilised.

However, in the winter of 1959, he was one of a number of Campbeltown fishermen who were asked to skipper and crew herring ring net vessels that had been acquired to hunt huge shoals off the Cork coast, sailing from Dunmore East, near Waterford. The local Irish fishermen had no knowledge of the method and were eager to be trained in its workings.

The success of the venture was to become the stuff of legend in the fishing community. My father skippered a boat called the *May 2* and his neighbour was my uncle, Tommy Ralston in the *Marie*. Constant heavy landings of good quality herring at excellent prices meant previously unheard of earnings for all.

A telegram boy delivered the money order to Ralston Road each Saturday evening at teatime and astronomical weekly wages of £80 and £90 were not uncommon throughout the three-month season. There was a marked improvement in the Clyde herring fishery shortly afterwards and some crews were earning steady money at the developing white fish and prawn trawling industry.

The following winter saw another exodus of herring fishermen to participate in the Eire Klondyke when my father and Uncle Tommy successfully skippered the *Glendalough* and the *Glenmalure*, two new 56-foot boats that were built specifically for the fishery by Tyrell of Arklow.

It was during this period of plenty that my mother purchased our first television set, a black and white 19-inch GEC model with sliding screen doors that cost £70. Before that joyous day, when televisions were still something of a rarity, viewing had been confined to visits to Auntie Martha's house in Crosshill Avenue or my friend Jim McIntyre's home a few doors away.

General Piped Television had just erected a mast at Crosshill Farm above the Meadows Estate in order to supply a common reception to subscribers, thus cutting out the need for a domestic aerial. Our new set was the first in Campbeltown to receive GPT reception and, to compensate for the frequent visits to the house by technicians attempting to fine tune the transmissions, we were given the service on a rental free basis for three months. I often heard my mother say that the cost of cleaning materials to tackle the floors and carpet after being trodden on by muddy boots probably amounted to more than the subscription fee!

Children's Hour was from 5pm until 6pm, and we were transfixed by the heroics of *Robin Hood, William Tell, Sir Lancelot* and *The Buccaneers*. Cowboy programmes included *The Cisco Kid, The Lone Ranger* and *Champion the Wonder Horse*. Other favourites were *The Whirlybirds, Crackerjack, Lassie, Hawkeye, Last of the* Mohicans, *The Railway Children* and the cartoon antics of *Popeye* and *Captain Pugwash*. We were allowed to watch some early evening westerns including *Rawhide, Laramie, Wagon Train* and *Wells Fargo*. On Friday nights, the curfew was extended to 9pm, which enabled us to see *Emergency Ward 10, Take Your Pick, Para Handy* and the hilarious *Army Game*.

Coverage of the Scottish football scene was in its infancy and prone to technical problems, but my friends and I were nevertheless enthralled by being able to actually *see* heroes like Bobby Evans, George Young, Willie Fernie, Jimmy Millar or Willie Bauld performing their magic. Before this, we had listened to big old-fashioned wireless sets as the distinctive voice of David Francie, one of Scotland's best-known commentators, described the action.

The advent of television into the house, of course, did not signal the end of outdoor activities and I was still to be found often in the usual retreats, as well as at the Scout Hall in John Street on Monday evenings, where the weekly meetings of the Wolf Cubs were held.

*

Some of my friends were issued with a set amount of pocket money on Saturday mornings, but my financial situation depended on a different method of cash accumulation. Each time I ran an errand for my mother, usually to Jack McRobert's shop, I was given 3d and, over the course of a week, was probably better off than my pals. On Saturday afternoons I was handed 1s 3d (slightly more than 6p) to pay for admission to the Rex Cinema film matinee, with instructions to buy a 1s ticket to the *better seats* and spend the remaining 3d on sweets. Needless to say, the cheapest ticket available, costing 8d, was chosen and the remaining 7d went on confections. I agonised over the decision whether to purchase a lasting toffee bar and caramels or blow 6d on an exotic chocolate fancy – plus consolation penny liquorice – that disappeared quickly!

There were periodic bonuses when, for instance, the Hydro Electric Board collector arrived to empty the domestic electricity meter, which was crammed with silver shilling and sixpenny coins. A rebate was given to householders and meter-emptying day guaranteed a bounty of a least one shilling from mother. Another windfall came in the form of a few shillings from the SCWS dividend, a similar type of rebate that was paid out to customers of the Co-operative at regular intervals. Mother often used the SCWS vans when they visited Ralston Road and was a regular visitor to its fancy goods and furniture store at Mafeking Place. Her dividend number of 1780 was written on a slip in a duplicate book, which was used to keep a record of all cash transactions. The only thing I disliked about the dividend payout was being sent to collect the money and having to stand in the inevitable long queue at the SCWS offices in Longrow.

Benevolent aunties and uncles, collecting empty lemonade bottles or doing odd jobs for neighbours were other sources of income. Helping to dismantle the temporary cattle and sheep pens at the conclusion of the Kintyre Agricultural Show, which in those days was held in June at High Kintyre Park, resulted in an original payment of five shillings; it rose, however, by annual increments in line with inflation!

Most of my pocket money was spent on sweeties, and the brands depended greatly on the fluctuating state of my finances. At the bottom end of the scale, a halfpenny could buy one little paper-wrapped caramel that was coated in chocolate. Bigger caramels in various flavours, gobstoppers, liquorice straps and large single *Mint Imperials* were available at 1d. Packets of chewing gum called *Beech Nut* and *PK*, *Puff Candy*, *Lucky Potatoes*, *Sherbet Dip* and

Refreshers cost 2d. For 3d, I could choose between treats such as *Spangles, Lucky Bags, Fruit Gums, McCowan's Highland Toffee* and two ounce bags of, for example, *Soor Plooms, Black Striped Balls, Acid Drops* or *Butternuts.* Sixpenny chocolate bars included *Dairy Milk, Mars, Tiffin, Nux* and *Jellimallo.*

A full-sized bottle of lemonade with rubber-sealed stone screwtop from either the Garvie or Dunn factories cost 1s, while the smaller metal-capped bottles retailed at 6d. Apart from the usual orange, lime and lemon flavours, there were other divine concoctions such as *Dunsade, Portobello, Red Kola, Appleade* and *American Cream Soda.* Lemonade and other soft drinks, especially Coca-Cola, were still something of a treat and I wonder at the comparison of consumption in Campbeltown nowadays, which, along with bottled water, must amount to thousands of gallons every week.

*

I was nine-years-old when I first experienced the excitement of herring ring net fishing on a trip aboard the *Stella Maris (CN 158)* with skipper Jim Meenan. Our neighbour was the *Regina Maris (CN 118),* skippered by Pat MacKay and the 55-foot green-painted McMillan of Fairlie-built vessels could be counted among the most successful in the fleet. That first night's work resulted in a shot of 60 baskets, which were landed at Tarbert, where the two boats lay during the daylight hours. A similar amount was caught the following night.

I will never forget the kindness shown to me by both Jim and his brother, Denis, who co-owned the vessel. When I think about it, they must have been really tolerant to agree to the repeated requests that allowed me to go to sea with them on so many occasions. I was truly saddened a few years later when Jim died at the young age of 42. The remainder of the *Stella Maris* crew, Joe Brown, Campbell McBrayne, Donald Munro and Jackie Paterson also made me feel welcome on the boat and often bought me treats in the landing ports of Ayr and Tarbert. I became familiar with lots of other fishermen, both young and old, and was soon able to identify them by their incredible nicknames, some examples of which were: *Dreesh; Gusbie; Scaivers; Neep; Sculla; Cactus; Sheepie; Klondyke; The World; Jake Boo.*

During my last year in Millknowe School, Uncle Tommy assumed command of the ringer *Nobles Again (CN 37)* and sailed in partnership with the Speed family's *Moira (CN 33)*. The two well-maintained varnished vessels, both powered by 114hp Gardner engines, drew many favourable comments in Campbeltown and other ports.

Uncle Tommy had long been one of my favourite relatives and it naturally followed that I was to be found aboard the *Nobles Again* frequently. The boat was originally intended to be a motor yacht when her keel was laid at the Gareloch yard of McGruer, but the decision to build a ring netter was made as work progressed and the 54-footer, coming as she did from a yacht builder, had many refinements not seen on other vessels in the fleet.

I suffered miserably from seasickness for a while and one night I lay under Uncle Tommy's tent-like duffel coat on the galley floor with a bucket at my head. I gradually got over the malady, though, and actually began to enjoy the rolling motion of the boat as she rounded Pladda in a south - westerly breeze, making for Ayr to land the herring.

When the *Nobles Again* was tied up for her refit in early June of that year, I rushed daily to the Old Quay from Millknowe School at four o'clock, where, amid the refreshing aroma of bilge cleaning detergent and newly applied varnish, I feasted on the remains of the teabreak chocolate biscuits while Uncle Tommy did my homework! The spruced-up boat went back to sea and my financial position was enhanced regularly on Saturdays by a payment of 3s 6d (seventeen and a half pence) from the boat's young cook, George McMillan, of Ardrishaig, for scrubbing out the forecastle at the end of the week's work; a covert operation that Uncle Tommy knew nothing about. George's seafaring career blossomed and he now sails as skipper of the MV *Calanus*, a marine research vessel based at the Marine Biological Research Station at Dunstaffnage, near Oban.

Early on Saturday mornings, when the crew had gone home, I savoured the raw smell of herring, tar and salt water given off by the recently used ring net. Inside the wheelhouse, I was conscious of a vague sterile tang created by methyl alcohol-impregnated Kelvin Hughes echo sounder recording paper, which had to be kept moist and in good condition in a round metal tin. I practised imaginary skilful berthing manoeuvres by emulating Uncle Tommy's simultaneous actions at the spokes of the shiny varnished steering wheel and big grey throttle lever, despite the fact that my eyes barely reached the level of the wheelhouse windows. I even enjoyed the stuffiness in the still warm forecastle, which was generated by fading heat waves from the dying Anthracite stove, mingled with vestiges of tobacco smoke and night-long human habitation. And I did not find in any way offensive the reek of engine room diesel and burned lubricating oil, coupled with the odour of a cooling Gardner engine. My shipboard chores over, an hour or so was spent catching *cuddies*, or, occasionally, a *Dougie Pole* - the Campbeltown name for an evil-looking little brown speckled fish that is said to be poisonous. Then it was off to High Kintyre Park for the weekly game of football.

My academic record in Millknowe was satisfactory, and although I was not destined to repeat the firsts of Primaries One and Two, my name was, nevertheless, to be found among the top five out of a class of 30 throughout my time there.

Football had always been important and that last year saw me donning the cherished black and yellow-striped shirt of the local senior boy's team, Glenside. I was further honoured when Mr. Beveridge, who also had an avid interest in soccer, handed me the captaincy of the school team. Our annual needle match with Dalintober at Kinloch Green, however, resulted in a narrow 2-1 win for the opposition – a scoreline that could easily have been 2-2. I am sure our right-winger, Alex (*Sauce*) Girvan, even after all those years, will remember the sitter he missed when, with the goalkeeper beaten and an open goal in front of him, he managed to slice the ball in the general direction of the War Memorial!

I had also developed into something of an athlete and was awarded the title of Millknowe School Sports Champion, Session 1961-62. In order to preserve amateur status, monetary sports prizes were handed out to successful competitors on the strict understanding that the cash was used to buy items such as books, games or toys. This was accomplished by a visit to Duncan Brown's Longrow shop, in the presence of a teacher who supervised the proceedings. My joy at becoming Sports Champion was marred somewhat when the accompanying female teacher (who shall remain nameless) made rather hurtful comments to me, including a reference to the "disgusting" amount of money I had to spend compared with the rest of the prize-winners. She was rather taken aback by an uncharacteristically truculent reply when I said that it wasn't my fault if the others could not run faster in the 80 and 120 yards sprints, or leap higher or longer in the jumping events, and I proceeded to spend the filthy lucre, which amounted to 12s 6d (62p).

I had been elevated from the Wolf Cubs to the Boy Scouts and, the day after I walked through Millknowe School's big green main doors for the very last time, I was among the boys of the 16th Argyll Troop who set off on annual summer camp to Logiealmond, near Perth.

I hardly missed a night at the ring net fishing during the remainder of the school holidays in the run-up to my enrolment at Campbeltown Grammar School. The *Nobles Again* and *Moira* were fishing well; but more importantly to me, Uncle Tommy had decided that my contributions of tea -making, scrubbing herring scales off the fish hold pound boards and collecting the boat's provisions merited a weekly remuneration of £1. The best shot of herring we had was one of 600 baskets, caught in three rings in Kilbrannan Sound between the Isle of Ross and Saddell Bay.

I had become fully accustomed to boat food and looked forward to the meals with relish. Even snacks, such as a dripping hot mutton pie and mug of strong tea taken at 2am, tasted wonderful. Sometimes the main meal when the boat was lying at Tarbert consisted of mountains of the famous Bruno's fish and chips and this once resulted in a chip eating competition between myself and Jim McIntyre – a contest fought with some fervour, I may add.

Easily the most memorable meal I ate on the *Nobles Again* was a magnificent fresh wild salmon salad, enjoyed as we lay at anchor in Skipness Bay during an early August day of that summer. The seven-pound fish had been caught along with the herring the previous night and was immediately attended to by Uncle Tommy, who was no mean hand at the stove, either, and I can still remember the precise method he used to cook it. He poured a copious quantity of a water/vinegar mixture (roughly 1/3 vinegar to 2/3 water) into a huge pot, before adding a generous pinch of salt. The salmon, minus head and tail, gutted and halved, was put into the cauldron, and brought to the boil. The heat was then turned down and the mixture simmered for exactly seven minutes before being taken off the cooker. The important step then, according to Uncle Tommy, was to allow the fish to stand in the liquid until completely cold before being removed, drained and placed on an ashet.

We ate it later, with a crisp summer salad and tomatoes, accompanied by buttered new potatoes (Uncle Tommy allowed me to smear a minimum amount of Heinz Salad Cream on mine!). The strawberries and Nestle's cream that followed may have come from tins, but the dessert set the seal on one of the finest boat dinners I have ever had.

Anyone who had the opportunity in those days of walking up a deserted Main Street, Campbeltown at five o'clock on a glorious summer morning - as I often did following my nights out at the fishing if the neighbour boat was away to market - would have savoured a seductive aroma that filled the surrounding area. This heavenly bouquet came from the premises of three bakeries, The SCWS, Hoyne and McArthur, as the first batches of morning rolls slid out of the big ovens. I sometimes called at the Hoyne bakehouse and bought half a dozen well-fired rolls to take home, and I usually ate a couple, still warm and spread with butter, before going to bed.

Some of my pals joined me now and again on nights out at the fishing but none of them could really understand the infinite enthusiasm I held for the life. It was on one of those occasions that two friends and myself carried out a desperate early morning act of bravado, which actually impressed nobody when the story was related later.

There was an apple tree at the rear of the offices of C. and D. Mactaggart, Solicitors, in Castlehill, which overhung the garden of one of the police houses directly opposite the police station. The plot was simple: we would pinch a few apples off the tree under the very noses of all branches of the law, a real act of daring even although it was 5am and the night officer in the police station was probably bent over his desk attending to paperwork. Stealthily, we crept like cats to the tree, where we each removed two small apples from the lower branches and made good our escape in an equally furtive manner. The spoils were sampled in Ralston Road, well past the police station, and the evil-tasting sourness of the rock hard crab apples was just reward for our illicit enterprise. The remains were jettisoned far into the field bordering the road, an ignominious end to an audacious raid that was never to be repeated.

I learned to swim that summer at the gently shelving Dalintober Beach, long before there was a swimming pool in the town. Diving off the mooring pontoons at the New Quay became a regular activity thereafter and my aquatic progress also meant that mother rubber-stamped my forays to Crosshill Loch, at the foot of Bengullion.

There had been past drowning tragedies at the fresh water loch and, as a non-swimmer, it was a no-go area, although clandestine visits had previously been made. We lit wood fires to warm us after swimming and chewed nuts picked from trees in the valley between the loch and Knockbay Farm.

*

I spent the first few hours of the 1962-63 session in Campbeltown Grammar School in a state of uncomfortable dampness, thanks to being on the receiving end of a traditional first year boy *ducking* at the hands of my brother, Robert and some of his third year cronies. Resplendent in immaculate uniform, I drank in the atmosphere of a whole new world in this voluminous and notable seat of learning that was established in 1686 - so different from the almost cosseted surroundings of Millknowe School. New friendships are created easily at that age and I made several, notably with Bobby Millar, Angus Graham, Neil MacPhail, John McKinlay and Roddy McKenzie. I was placed in Knockscalbert House and, much to my delight, was picked for the football team for the weekly inter-house games, an honour shared by Bobby. We also played for the school team, with varying results, against sides from other parts of Argyll and the Glasgow area, but I have difficulty in erasing the painful memory of a 7-1 thrashing we received away from home at the hands of Royal Albert High School, Clydebank, in the Scottish Schools Cup in November of that year.

As the weeks passed, I gauged the friendliness – or otherwise – of the teaching staff and, with one unquestionable female exception, I enjoyed going to their classes. Every schoolboy has his favourite teachers and mine were very definitely John McKerral, Helen Martindale and Ronnie Togneri; though generally speaking I liked most of the others.

John McKerral was our geography teacher, a genial man who seldom lost his temper. His teaching skills were considerable and he was a most interesting man to listen to. John kept a well-used Black of Lochgelly leather tawse in his desk – an instrument of torture he referred to as *Horace*. Punishment was dispensed according to the severity of the classroom offence, and could range from a gentle tap (usually reserved for the girls) to a fairly hefty wallop. I was on the fully justified receiving end of *Horace* several times but I suspect that John did not really enjoy doling out this type of corrective action as he could easily have used more force.

Helen Martindale (later Mrs Togneri) was a newly qualified teacher who took us for French. I think it was because I knew Helen previously in her native Carradale - also my mother's home village - and the fact that she wore trendy 1960's clothes that endeared me so much to her. She was a true expert in her field, though, and I still retain a basic knowledge of the French language after all this time, despite the fact that I have never used it in earnest since my schooldays. Being a young teacher, Helen's tawse was brand new and hard as teak. One experience of her belt was quite enough for me for, petite as she was, Helen could administer the necessary punishment effortlessly. The fact that she also threatened to tell my mother (which she never did) about my misdemeanour ensured impeccable behaviour from then on.

Ronnie was, in the early days of Beatlemania, our hero. He had the courage to challenge the establishment and come to school as a youthful art teacher dressed in semi winkle-picker shoes, natty Italian suits and wearing his hair at below collar length. Ronnie's methods of teaching the rudiments of art to this completely untalented individual were done in such a way that I have never forgotten much of what he imparted in the Grammar School nearly 40 years ago. Ronnie also showed an interest in the herring fishing and often went out with his friend, Donald Munro, on the *Stella Maris*, another reason why he was high on my popularity list. Ronnie's romance with Helen blossomed and we nosy pupils followed its progress with interest until the couple later married, much to our delight.

I am glad to say that my three favourite former teachers are still around in the town. I was certainly no model pupil and perhaps prone to a certain amount of devilment, but I hope they will agree that I wasn't a teenage rebel, hell bent on making life miserable for my mentors.

*

Not long after I started secondary school life, I became message boy in McArthur's Union Street bakery shop. Brother Robert previously held the position but had moved on to a better-paid appointment in Michael Brodie's ironmongery store. Rolls were delivered between the hours of 7am and 8am from Robbie McArthur's van, since it would have been impossible to service the very many orders to both the Meadows and Calton estates by bicycle. I reported back to the shop at 4pm each weekday except Wednesday for another hour's work, this time using pedal power on the big black delivery bike, which took me to all parts of the town. Saturday's hours were from 7am-8am and from 10am until 4pm; all for the princely sum of £1:5s per week (£1: 25p).

However, this steady income, minus a small contribution to the household, meant that I could arrange my finances with a semblance of order, though impulsive buying of little personal effects sometimes resulted in a shortfall before pay day.

Two months into my Grammar scholarship, I was introduced to the dubious and illegal pleasures of a nearby billiard hall known in Campbeltown as *The Jack*. Truth to tell, I became completely hooked on snooker and made many illicit visits to this forbidden establishment, which was very much out of bounds to Grammar schoolboys, though the kindly attendants, Hector Gilchrist and Bob Sinclair, turned a blind eye to the school ruling.

A betting game called *Skittles*, which incorporated five little wooden pins – four brown and one black - arranged around the table centre spot, was played by anything up to twelve players. The game's rules followed standard billiard scoring, but at least one of the brown pins had to be knocked over, the value of which was included in the winning score of 17 points. If the black pin was overturned, then the player concerned was automatically disqualified. Each competitor paid the eventual victor a pre-arranged stake, which was usually one shilling (5p), and winning a few games could make a healthy profit for the cueman. As I became more proficient at the table, I took part in regular *Skittles* sessions and collected my fair share of winnings. However, extra-curricular activities such as regular visits to *The Jack*, Rex Cinema or other evening diversions, allowed by my mother only after I had given her the totally false impression that all necessary homework had been completed, resulted in a downturn in my scholastic performance. I also seemed to lose interest in academic matters and was more concerned about the latest developments on the pop music scene. I only realised in later years how much I must have disappointed my parents, especially after having done so well in Millknowe School but I did, however, eventually buckle down and results did improve dramatically.

Towards the end of the 1962-63 session at The Grammar, I acquired a habit that was to take me 29 long years to finally forego, when I inhaled my first puff of cigarette smoke. Robert and his friend, Brian Sharp, were about to leave school and had become established smokers, along with many other senior pupils of both sexes who could be found during break times at secret hideouts in the school grounds. On the day in question, I pestered Robert and Brian relentlessly to let me try a few draws and they gave in, but added an ominous condition: "Inhale it or yer gettin' buffed," which was a Campbeltown way of warning me that I must swallow the smoke or suffer the consequences! Their orders were carried out to the letter and, as happens in so many similar experiments, I was destined to become a slave to the *weed*.

Smoking was to get me into trouble twice at school, the first time when I was caught red-handed by art teacher John Crawford as he walked past the rear of the dining hall. He took me straight to the rector, Hector MacKenzie, who administered six strokes of the belt and, even worse, sent a letter to my parents informing them of the heinous crime. On the second occasion, I was having a fly puff in the boys' toilets at the Wee Grammar when janitor Alec Burnfield walked in completely out of the blue. Despite my protestations that Alec lived a mere two doors from my family in Ralston Road and was a boyhood friend of my father, he insisted in accompanying me to the dreaded Hector's office yet again. Alec marched me to within inches of the rector's study and actually went through the motions of preparing to knock on the door with balled fist before he withdrew his hand and said with barely disguised glee: "I'll bet ye were shakin' in yer shoes there, Freddy!" Incidentally, when I reached adulthood, I sometimes met Alec in a bar and the inevitable reference to my great escape usually cost me a pint of beer.

Another painful punishment occurred in Ralston Road, when Jim McIntyre's mother, Jessie, saw us smoking in the field at the rear of the houses. Give Jessie her due, she asked me if I wished to be dealt with there and then, or at home after she had informed my mother of the circumstances. I quickly opted for the former, whereupon Jim and I each received a stinging blow on the backside, Jessie's weapon being one of the old-fashioned clover-shaped cane carpet beaters that many housewives used in those days.

It goes without saying that there were very many occasions when I could not raise the amount of money necessary for even the cheapest of cigarette packs (five Cadets retailed at 8d - slightly more than 3p). In consequence, along with a number of my of my mates, regular visits were made to The Tobacco House in Main Street, where a single tipped cigarette could be purchased for 3d from a specially-opened packet, although in the eyes of the law, the deal was one of complete illegality.

I actually got out of the Grammar two weeks before the session ended that year, being one of a party of Campbeltown schoolchildren who took part in a school cruise aboard the MV *Devonia*, a B.I. Line ship that had been converted for the purpose. We joined schools from all over Scotland and Ireland at the Greenock Ocean Terminal and enjoyed a fantastic two-week trip to the Baltic Scandinavian countries and Russia, and stories emanating from the experience were related for months afterwards. We were supposed to have had classroom sessions as we sailed between the various destinations to make up for the lost school time, but our teachers in charge generously allowed us more or less complete freedom.

*

When Robert left school to go to the herring fishing, I succeeded him as message boy job in Michael Brodie's shop. Michael was a very benevolent man and the weekly wage packet of £2:10s (£2:50) was the envy of all my errand boy friends. I only worked one hour each day (Wednesday's excepted) after school and Saturday shop opening hours. My main duty was delivering Esso Blue paraffin in gallon or two-gallon cans to the many customers who had oil heaters. A drawback was that the shop did not have a custom-built message bike, and I had to balance the containers precariously on the handlebars of an ordinary pedal cycle whilst steering with one hand. During the holidays I worked full-time shop hours, helping out behind the counter, and the remuneration went up to an incredible £5 per week. Michael's son, Neil, played drums for *The Sceptres*, and I often accompanied him to impromptu practice sessions after work. My healthy financial position enabled me to be out and about on most nights with friends during the summer holidays and we were beginning to take more than a passing interest in girls. The fairground on Kinloch Green was a favourite gathering place, where we listened to the reverberating sounds of artistes including the

Rolling Stones, Hollies, or P.J. Proby. Clumsy efforts were made to secure the affections of our particular fancies, the occasional successful outcome being an assignation at The Rex – carried out under a cloak of secrecy lest parents find out.

My interest in children's television had waned and I looked forward instead to watching the antics of comedians of the calibre of *Francie and Josie, Dick Emery, Morecambe and Wise,* or *Arthur Haynes.* Police dramas included *Z-Cars, No Hiding Place* and *Dixon of Dock Green,* while medical productions such as *Dr. Kildare* or *Doctor Finlay's Casebook* also drew huge viewing figures. On the pop scene, David Jacobs hosted *Juke Box Jury* on BBC before being replaced by *Top of the Pops,* while ITV offered *Ready Steady Go* and *Thank Your Lucky Stars.* Considerable technical advances in the coverage of football had been made and I was an avid fan of the *Scotsport* team of Arthur Montford, Alex Cameron and Bob Crampsey.

I was by no means a television addict, though, and most of my free time was spent outdoors, especially playing football at High Kintyre Park on clear nights. Further new companionships were developed during the unofficial games and I became friendly with three older lads, Jack (*Hibs*) McGeachy, Angus Brodie and James Lafferty. *Hibs,* with his short and stocky physique, was particularly skilled at dribbling and his play resembled the weaving antics of Celtic and Scotland's national hero, Jimmy Johnstone.

We often combined short summer games of football with other leisure pursuits such as boat hiring or a visit to the putting green. *Hibs* may have been an excellent footballer but he displayed an alarming lack of basic navigational skills one evening in Campbeltown Loch as we cruised around on board one of John Shields' little motor boats, the *Osprey.* He was at the helm when the boat struck a pipeline concrete junction box that had just been covered by the rising tide and the marine ply planking suffered damage. Although we were only yards offshore, panic set in when ingress of water was noticed and *Hibs* steered the boat for the beach, where we disembarked. The *Osprey* was made fast to the sea wall railing and we made off for home with understandable rapidity along the Limecraigs cutting, too terrified to face John's wrath. Worrying days ensued until we eventually found out that the *Osprey* had suffered only minor damage and had been quickly repaired. More importantly, far from being angry, John was pleased that we had the sense to beach the boat and secure it safely. Boat hiring excursions were, therefore, resumed immediately.

Before one of our regular evening games of putting, *Hibs* dangerously suggested that, in order to make the outcome more interesting, the player with the highest score should be penalised by having to pitch his ball into Campbeltown Loch. Excuses suggesting the ball had mysteriously been lost would be offered to the attendant, Bob Benson, and payment made to cover the cost of a replacement. The five-strong group of youthful putters showed intense concentration during the 18-hole contest and the carefully recorded number of strokes resulted in none other than *Hibs* himself having to carry out the naughty deed! Needless to say, the sum paid over to Bob at the putting green hut later was reason enough for *Hibs* to call for an immediate end to that particular caper.

I have to say that I enjoyed life as the 1960's rolled on. John McKinlay and I were regular attenders at the junior dances held on Friday nights in Babbette Stevenson's High Street premises. I seldom missed a Sunday night at the Christian Institute Youth Club, either.

When we were 15, John and I had a fine holiday with his Auntie Nan and Uncle Frank when they lived in the Leicestershire village of Sileby, the first time we had crossed the border. Another *first* during the weeklong stay saw us tasting beer in a quaint little English pub, an experience I found, strangely, to be something of a non-event. Although my herring fishing trips had been drastically curtailed due to work commitments in Michael's shop, I was still to be found at the Old Quay frequently. Campbeltown was becoming increasingly popular as a landing port by prawn fishermen from Portavogie, Northern Ireland, and I forged many lifelong friendships with younger crewmen on the Belfast registered boats.

*

Session 1965-66 was to be my last in Campbeltown Grammar School, though I did not know this until I was almost due to begin another term at the end of the summer holidays.

During that last year, marked academic improvements continued to be made, much to the relief of my parents - especially mother, a particularly intelligent Grammar School pupil who had dealt effortlessly with such complicated subjects as the Greek Classics.

I was still easily coerced into mischievous episodes of a frivolous nature, but which nevertheless caused some teachers a certain amount of grief. We got our *kicks* out of living, and not from pills, needles or lighter fuel cans. How I wish that youngsters in today's drugs-riddled society could travel back in time to those wonderful years, when the most powerful stimulants known to us came in the form of either a cup of coffee or glass of Coca-Cola.

I created minor mayhem in Miss Renee McGougan's maths class immediately following the lunch break one day when I tried to hide a small terrier dog in my desk. The little Westie had followed me to school and resisted all efforts to drive him homeward. In my ignorance, I agreed to a suggestion from a friend that the lidded desk with a convenient air hole in its base would provide ideal refuge for him until the bell rang for break time, when I could return the animal to its owner in nearby Range Road.

Naturally, only minutes had elapsed before Miss McGougan was made fully aware of the dog's presence as ear-splitting yelps echoed around the classroom and I was sent out with instructions to see that the dog was delivered safely home. On my return, she handed me a note detailing the circumstances and told me to take it personally to the rector, whom, she was sure, would deal with me accordingly. To my unbelievable relief, Hector MacKenzie saw the funny side of it all and I escaped unpunished!

The mini-skirt had well and truly arrived and we boy pupils in the mixed class ogled with delight as we decided which girl to ply with amateurish charm. Along with my friends, I experienced the heart-fluttering stirrings of a new teenage romance, usually initiated by the passing of secret notes in class. Conversely, I also endured the emotional agony suffered when a girl decided to end it and usually spent a few days brooding before regaining the confidence to start afresh!

At the conclusion of Session 1965-66, I was once again involved in a school trip, this time to Germany's Rhineland. I was proud of the fact that careful saving of some of my shop wages enabled me to pay for the holiday myself, which the 30-strong party enjoyed greatly. It was the first time I had flown abroad, albeit in an ancient DC-4 from RAF Manston, in Kent; it was, nevertheless, an interesting experience!

I had a gut feeling that I would not be going back to classes in Campbeltown Grammar School and, on returning from Germany, I noticed a job advertisement in the local newspaper that appealed to me. Following a successful interview with editor Gordon Lang, my boyhood effectively ended on August 22, 1966, when I joined the staff of *The Campbeltown Courier* as a junior reporter. But that is another story.

THE FUTURE

Who could have forecast a few short decades ago that The Royal Burgh of Campbeltown would decline to such a degree? Instead of marching into its Tercentenary as the proud, prosperous industrial town that I grew up in, it has the unenviable distinction of being one of the country's worst economic and unemployment blackspots, a situation so thoroughly and sadly emphasised by the profusion of boarded up shops, offices and pubs. At the time of writing – early 2000 - the unemployment figure is 36% higher than the rest of Argyll.

Campbeltown has staggered from one crisis to another, brought upon the town not by any fault of its people, but by an ongoing set of unfortunate circumstances. The last 12-month period has, unbelievably, seen 53 of 150 businesses closing down.

We shall never again see a newly built steel seine-netter/trawler, renowned for its sea-keeping qualities and preferred by the country's top fishing skippers, slide into Campbeltown Loch from the slipway of the now almost derelict Campbeltown Shipyard.

The few inshore prawn boats that lie against the Old Quay bear testimony to a drastically reduced fishing fleet. The astronomical cost of fishing licences, plus lack of government financial support, have combined to effectively prohibit keen young fishermen from buying into the industry.

The trawl nets so vital to the remaining Campbeltown fishermen no longer come from the once thriving premises of Joseph Gundry or Flaws and Shaw, ironically situated only a few yards from the head of the Old Quay in Kinloch Road, but from places as distant as Fleetwood, Musselburgh or Peterhead.

Whisky distilling, when 34 plants were in production, provided many jobs in the town. The two distilleries that are, thankfully, still operating, will certainly not be augmented by further expansion in the foreseeable future, given the present problems facing whisky producers.

The Argyll Colliery at Machrihanish, where 200 miners once broke honest sweat, will never yield another ounce of coal. Only memories remain of this once productive pit that provided so much work. And the mothballing of the base at RAF Machrihanish was another body blow that effectively removed an estimated £1.4 million annually from the local economy.

Skilled joiners, bricklayers, painters and electricians look in vain for work as long days spent in a seemingly endless dark tunnel drag slowly onwards.

Campbeltonians, though, are a resilient lot and surely it is now appropriate to fight back before any further depressing developments turn the place into a true ghost town.

I would contend that Campbeltown's downward slide was accelerated in the 1970's, when local government reorganisation swept the country and Campbeltown Town Council was disbanded. The reinstatement of a full Town Council with its attendant pomp and ceremony is impracticable, but I would suggest that a radical local government reshuffle is necessary for the efficient running of Argyll's three main burghs, especially Campbeltown.

I think the answer lies in the appointment of a realistically paid seven-man Executive, answerable to Argyll and Bute Council, to look after the affairs of towns with a population in excess of 5000, i.e. Dunoon, Oban and Campbeltown. The rest of the Argyll and Bute area would remain under the control of the Council's Kilmory headquarters.

Attractive salaries could be offered to professionals with a proven record in their respective fields of law, engineering, accountancy and leisure. The remaining three members of the Executive would be equally qualified persons from the business world.

An annual budget geared to meet the burghs' needs would have to made available to the Executive, this body being fully accountable for its expenditure.

Once up and running, the priority of the Executive would have to be the creation of jobs, which, in turn, would give people back their dignity. It is now time to forget about traditional industries and join the electronic roller coaster and a massive effort should be made to establish a major call centre or something similar in Campbeltown. Geographical location means little in the modern world of communications and, indeed, an attractive area such as the South Kintyre district could well be conducive to a favourable decision by a national concern to set up in Campbeltown.

Something must also be done with the ro-ro ferry linkspan at the New Quay. Even the greatest optimist will concede that the Campbeltown-Ballycastle ferry service has not exactly been an unqualified success and it is unlikely ever to be a money-spinning route, despite claims to the contrary.

I do not lay the blame on anyone in particular but the fact that the costly berthing facility lies unused for the greater part of the year prompts me to suggest that it could be utilised for alternative purposes, running to a regular timetable. A glaring example is the transportation of timber to the Ayrshire coast by a suitable vessel, which would remove many of the trundling juggernauts from the totally unsuitable A83 road. Obviously, car and passenger traffic from both directions should also be encouraged on board. Livestock and other commodities could also easily be transported by sea, especially since anti-pollution awareness is now an uppermost consideration.

I would go along with a recent suggestion that RAF Machrihanish should be used as a long-haul flight-refuelling stop by Eastern Bloc countries. Once established, other feasible proposals such as the setting up of an air freight depot could be submitted. After all, a figure approaching £14m was spent on its refurbishment not that long ago and the main runway is reputed to be the second longest in Europe. The landing facility, alone, being able to accommodate the largest aircraft in the world, is an asset that is ripe for exploitation.

Tourism, naturally, will always be actively promoted, but only when a substantial number of jobs have been created and money is once again being spent in Campbeltown's reopened shops and pubs would thoughts turn to leisure and entertainment.

There are ways of attracting tourists to Campbeltown; the immediate area abounds with fine land and seascapes, beaches and golf courses and this provides an ideal platform from which to start. However, well-publicised amenities need to be in place also, in order to bring people to the town.

One big step in this direction would be the creation of a major maritime museum, an establishment with the necessary criteria to attract lottery funding. It should be done properly, of course, with a hands-on collection of floating exhibits incorporating, for example, an ex-Royal Navy submarine, fishing trawler, RNLI lifeboat and coasting vessel, as well as interesting smaller craft.

One need look no further than the suitably sheltered waters of Campbeltown Loch as a site for such a venture; perhaps something could be done in the area of the largely unused NATO jetty. A separate building for smaller displays, nautical memorabilia and a decent restaurant could easily be erected in the immediate vicinity. Such a museum, if properly promoted, could well be the ideal magnet for drawing people to the area, even during the winter months to a lesser extent.

Obviously, to sustain the holidaymakers' interest, other attractive facilities would have to be available.

The famous Davaar Island cave painting of the Crucifixion, which has been seen by many thousands during the last century, is a perfect example of a potentially valuable tourism asset. A small steel vessel, with bow-loading ramp of the type seen at fish farms, could be utilised to ferry up to twelve passengers per sailing, embarking at either the north side of the Old Quay or from a specially built slipway at the Kilkerran side of the Dhorlinn. At convenient states of the tide, passengers would be able to walk directly off the boat on to the Dhorlinn. I am sure that other uses could be found around the harbour for such a boat during off-peak times.

Remaining on a nautical theme, there is surely still an opening for small boat hiring, fishing trips and even diving charters, utilising a larger vessel such as a converted MFV. There is room for additional yacht berthing facilities in the inner harbour and extra moorings at the Dalintober anchorage.

The once golden sandy curve of Dalintober Beach is now a barren shingle and stone strewn crescent. It was the brainchild of the late Councillor William Stevenson, who many years ago convinced the Town Council to create the beach by transporting thousands of tons of sand to Dalintober. Countless children spent untold hours of joy at play on the sands or in the safe waters that skirted the beach. It has, however, been sadly neglected in recent years and now needs drastic regeneration.

The broad greensward that runs the length of Kilkerran Promenade is a particularly pleasant area of Campbeltown, and which, in my opinion, should remain so. Plans have been drawn up for a bold £1m-plus leisure and entertainment complex on the site but I would hold that the scheme is somewhat over ambitious.

However, I would like to see the reinstatement of the two putting greens and the provision of an unobtrusive miniature railway line alongside the paving that stretches from the ferry terminal to the children's' play area at the former paddling pool. Strategically placed picnic tables, the replacement of the formerly well used shelters and the setting up once again of the *fairy lights* would also enhance the promenade.

The large area of Kinloch Green between John Street and the Esplanade War Memorial is a perfect location for a pitch and putt course, an attraction with appeal for both local people and holidaymakers.

The display in Campbeltown's Heritage Centre - the former Lorne Street Church building - is a credit to the group that runs the place and provides an excellent supplement to the Campbeltown Museum. However, something must be done about the unkempt appearance of the weed-bound gravel grounds surrounding the centre. A new welcoming signboard would not go amiss, either, and a purpose-built cafeteria would probably bring in valuable extra income.

Maybe it is also time to turn the clock back and add to the two main annual events of today – the Highland Games and the Music Festival – by the reintroduction of a Civic Week, organised on a format similar to that used 40 years ago. A week packed with many different activities would culminate on Saturday afternoon, when a newly elected *Miss Campbeltown* would lead an imaginative and substantial lorry tableaux. Following a water sports programme and fishing boat trips in the evening, the day would end by the staging of a special '60's' night dance in the Victoria Hall.

Golf is one of the world's most popular participation sports and Campbeltown is fortunate in that there are four courses within easy reach of the town, including the Isle of Gigha's nine hole delight. Golfing breaks, therefore, with alternative diversions for *golf widows* should be organised and promoted enthusiastically.

Anyone who has ever enjoyed a foreign package holiday knows that coach tours to places of interest are popular with tourists. Why not here? An imaginative day trip taking in visits to places such as St Columba's Footsteps, Dunaverty Rock, the UK reception site at Machrihanish of the world's first transatlantic radio transmission, the well preserved ancient fort at Kildonan and the picturesque fishing village of Carradale could well be the forerunner of other equally interesting tours. Kintyre has many splendid little eating houses, any one of which could be chosen for the obligatory lunch stop. And the beautiful Isle of Gigha, with its stunning Achamore Gardens, lovely little white sandy beaches and award winning hotel, is only a short ferry ride away.

Shopkeepers in the revitalised Campbeltown would also have to play an important part by following the example of their Oban counterparts, who long ago gave up the traditional lunchtime and half-day closing, though I suspect they would be rather willing to do so if things turned for the better. Hoteliers, too, would be expected to come up with attractively priced deals with dining room menus featuring fresh Campbeltown seafood, other local produce and perhaps the inclusion of a whisky tasting evening and distillery visits. Surely some real development on this subject can evolve from the fact that, in December 1999, Campbeltown's very own Springbank Malt Whisky was awarded the distinction of being the finest in the world, an accolade of which I, as a Campbeltonian, am unreservedly proud of.

Apart from the completely off-putting sight of so many commercial premises lying idle, the town itself needs to be brought into line with similar sized burghs, which have made their town centres so much more appealing. The pedestrianisation of Longrow South and Reform Square is an absolute necessity. And the provision of a traffic light controlled Zebra Crossing in Main Street, created to extend a vehicle free Longrow South, would ensure safe pedestrian passage to the other side of the main thoroughfare. This arrangement would cause little disruption to the town's traffic flow and, as any driver knows, would eliminate the present nightmare of attempting a right turn on to Main Street.

In conclusion, it is my heartfelt hope that the buoyant and friendly Royal Burgh of Campbeltown of my youth will re-emerge and once more become an economic force to be reckoned with in Argyll. True Campbeltonians are resolute people, but the Scottish Executive must help by showing genuine commitment aimed at reversing the fortunes of this troubled town.

June 2000